aRe We THeRe Yet?

Don't Miss the eBook

*Are We There Yet? A Modern American Family's Cross Country
Adventures,* is also published as an "eBook" and your purchase
of this printed edition entitles you to download
the free Electronic Edition in Adobe Software's PDF Format.
The Electronic Edition is identical in appearance to the
printed edition you now hold in your hands, but all
Internet hyperlinks are active—a simple click
will take you to the Website mentioned.
In addition, the Table of Contents, Subject Index and
complete Appendix of Websites are also hyperlinked.

For download instructions, please register your copy of
Are We There Yet?
at:

http://awty.webpointers.com

For Connie & Jack –
Wishing you
safe and happy travels!
Bill Lohmann
10/2/15

aRe We THeRe Yet?

A Modern American Family's Cross-Country Adventure

by Bill Lohmann

An original WebPointers™ Interactive Internet Guide
Published by Hope Springs Press

http://www.webpointers.com

Portions of this work appeared originally in the Richmond Times-Dispatch, and
they are reproduced by permission of the Richmond Times-Dispatch.

ISBN 0-9639531-7-6

Library of Congress Catalogue Card Number - 00-112153

1 2 3 4 5 6 7 8 9 0

An Original *WebPointers™* Interactive Internet Guide

Contents

For Robin, Melissa, Alexandra and Jack.

Thanks for the ride.

Preface: planning this excellent adventure

When I told people that I would spend seven weeks driving across America and back with my wife and three children, the initial response was generally the same:

"You're doing *what?*"

Followed quickly by:

"Have you lost your mind?"

And so it was with such widespread support that we left town and embarked on our once-in-a-lifetime adventure (by our standards, anyway) to discover America and determine, once and for all, whether we could actually set up a tent and sleep in it.

As it turned out, we could.

But not particularly well.

This was a cross between "National Lampoon's Vacation" and "The Brady Bunch" with a

Robin, Alex, Melissa, Jack & Bill Lohmann

smattering of "Fear and Loathing in Las Vegas" thrown in for good measure. While we were preparing to leave, a newspaper colleague kindly analyzed that our trip had all the makings of "a really scary movie."

Boo.

In fact, before we left, I wavered between sheer excitement and outright fear. I knew the trip had the potential to be the greatest thing our family had ever done or ever might do. I also knew it could be a complete fiasco.

It turned out to be the greatest thing we'd ever done, and only a partial fiasco.

We lived to tell the tale. And I imagine we'll be telling it for years to come.

... a cross between "National Lampoon's Vacation" and "The Brady Bunch" with a smattering of "Fear and Loathing in Las Vegas" ...

An Original *Web*Pointers™ Interactive Internet Guide

The idea for this adventure was mine and mine alone (although I received prior approval from my wife Robin before actually submitting the proposal). So, I take full responsibility.

It was the summer of 1999, annual budget request time at the Richmond Times-Dispatch, where I work as a feature writer and columnist. Each summer, we must submit funding requests for special projects for the following year. Submitting is easy — it's not hard to dream up ways to spend other people's money — but gaining approval is another story.

Unfazed, I suggested a cross-country family vacation for the summer of 2000.

This was not an utterly shameless pitch for a subsidized vacation. It was merely shameless. We would pay part of our way and I would work the entire way, writing stories, shooting photographs, corresponding with readers through a Web site that would be constructed for the trip.

And this project was not far from my beat at the paper. I've written about family issues for several years, including a few stories about families who have traveled together extensively. In interviewing those families, I was always intrigued not only by the interesting places they had visited and the experiences they had shared, but also by how they managed not to kill each other along the way.

This being the dawn of a new millennium, I suggested, what better way to usher in a new age than with the old tradition — old, at least, by late 20th century standards — of a family vacation?

My editors bought the idea.

I let out a satisfying sigh. Then I got scared.

It's a bit fanciful to consider taking a long, complicated trip. Reality sets in, though, when you sit down with a calendar and try to figure out how far you will drive each day, what you will see and where you will sleep (and, in my case, what I would write about and where I would plug in all of the electronic gadgets necessary to do my job). Throw three kids in the back — their needs, their wants, their proclivity for motion sickness — and the task becomes truly daunting.

Robin and I have three children: Melissa, 13 (she became a teenager in Texas), Alexandra, 7, and Jack, 4. Ideally, Jack would have been a little older before we attempted such a journey — and, ideally, gas prices wouldn't have been so high. But life is not often ideal and you take the opportunity when it is presented.

We began making plans in January, nearly six months before we would leave, and we did something trip-related almost every day until we pulled out of our driveway on July 1.

... life is not often ideal and you take the opportunity when it is presented.

We bought a new atlas, we purchased several books about national parks and scenic highways, and we talked to families who had taken cross-country trips. We acquired trip-making computer software. We started prowling the World Wide Web, which would prove to be an indispensable tool.

Then we had to determine the route we would take. We always assumed we would go out across the northern tier of the United States and come back through the South. Somehow, we knew we wanted to spend a few days toward the end of our trip on the white-sand beaches along the Gulf of Mexico. We thought we would need it. We were right.

We also knew we could not do the entire country. Seven weeks is a long time, but not that long. Early on, we decided to forget about the Northeast. Nothing against the Northeast, but we wanted to see places that were new to us, which primarily meant most everything west of the Mississippi River.

That settled, we committed our first official trip-planning act. I convinced Robin to allow me to purchase tickets — in February — to a baseball game: the St. Louis Cardinals vs. the Cincinnati Reds, in St. Louis, on the afternoon of the Fourth of July. The Cardinals have been my favorite team since my father told me they were when I was a kid.

Besides St. Louis, there were a number of other places we absolutely knew we wanted to visit: Yellowstone, Glacier and Grand Canyon national parks; the states of California, New Mexico and Texas. We wanted to play catch on the ball field carved from the Iowa farm where "Field of Dreams" was filmed, and stand on a corner in Winslow, Arizona. We wanted to set foot, if only for a few hours, in Canada and Mexico. We wanted to dip our toes in the Pacific Ocean and the Gulf of Mexico. Along the way, we would stumble onto unexpected gems: an annual chicken festival in Nebraska, a guest ranch in Idaho and an exotic animal ranch in Washington, among others.

All in all, we had a long way to go and a short time to get there.

The newspaper provided me an expense budget, but not carte blanche. We were operating on a per diem basis that we knew from the outset would not cover all of our expenses. So, we were careful to count our nickels.

We were very fortunate with our mode of transportation. Because I was on assignment from the newspaper, I was able to work through the Recreational Vehicle Industry Association and lease a conversion van from Vanworks Inc., a van conversion company in Fort Collins, Colo.

We started prowling the World Wide Web, which would prove to be an indispensable tool.

An Original *Web*Pointers™ Interactive Internet Guide

The van was a dark blue GMC Savana, a powerful machine equipped with two CD players, a DVD player and a VCR. A liquid-crystal-display video monitor unfolded from the ceiling. The back seat reclined into a bed (although we were packed too tight to ever use it as one). The van came with a portable vacuum cleaner, a flashlight and a generous air-conditioning system. The upholstery was leather and the accommodations comfortable and spacious, although we filled it up in a hurry with our belongings. We also packed a lot of faith in it.

We needed to give it a name. John Steinbeck, in "Travels With Charley," named his camper Rocinante. Hunter Thompson had the Great Red Shark in "Fear and Loathing in Las Vegas." We dubbed the van, Big Blue. (After seven weeks in Big Blue, our minivan will forever be known as Little Green.)

It would have been nice to have climbed aboard Big Blue and allowed the open road to take us wherever it wished. Unplanned and unfettered. But with three kids to consider and deadlines to meet, it wouldn't have been practical. We drew up a fairly rigid itinerary and made lodging reservations in most places before we left Richmond.

We also bought a tent.

We love the outdoors — the beach, the mountains, the ball fields — but we're not big on sleeping out there. Particularly me. I think Holiday Inns were created for a reason.

But we couldn't afford to stay in motels everywhere and frankly we wanted a taste of the camping experience, so we bought a tent, praying it would not rain and the bears would not eat us.

We first set up the five-person tent in our garage for a dress rehearsal. One evening after dinner a few weeks before we were scheduled to leave, everyone laid out their sleeping bags in the tent and got all snuggled in. Then I turned out the lights. The good times lasted about 30 seconds. One child bounced, one child complained, one just wanted to be next to his mommy. I quickly turned on the lights and retired inside to contemplate what I had wrought.

Someone asked if we planned to have an actual outdoor "practice" camping trip before we left. No way, I told them. I didn't want to know how bad it was going to be. I'd prefer it remain a mystery.

We upgraded our AAA membership, acquired numerous AAA TourBooks and made arrangements for a TripTik, which offers route recommendations. We used the Rand McNally TripMaker and StreetFinder software, which provided driving times, distances and routes between destina-

We love the outdoors — the beach, the mountains, the ball fields — but we're not big on sleeping out there. Particularly me. I think Holiday Inns were created for a reason.

tions, as well as places to stay and eat. It also generated a pretty cool map with our route emblazoned on it.

We visited our local libraries, checking out numerous books for bedtime on a variety of reading levels. Long before we left our kids had a good sense of Lewis and Clark, Mark Twain, the Alamo, the Grand Canyon and other historic figures and places we would encounter.

I cannot imagine planning a trip this extensive without using the World Wide Web. We researched places, made lodging arrangements, and initiated contact with people we wound up meeting along the way. It was stunningly easy, and we did it mostly on our time and at our convenience, usually late at night after the kids were in bed.

Planning a long trip today is certainly different than planning a similar trip a generation or two ago. I listen to friends my age talk about cross-country trips they took as kids with their families: station wagons loaded to the gills, all-night rides, hard-to-manage tents pitched in a new place every day, the entire feat requiring only two or three weeks.

I am in awe. But I am not jealous. I mean, I can admire what Lewis and Clark accomplished without wishing I could have gone along for the ride. I enjoyed being able to remove some of the mystery about what's out there by using tools, such as the Web, not available to generations past. I was ecstatic at having a large vehicle to tote us and our stuff. I was even mildly pleased to have a tent that could be set up in only a few minutes. And I wouldn't have wanted to attempt a trip of this magnitude in anything less than seven weeks. We felt rushed, as it was.

Technological advances also were critical for our trip. Because I was writing and shooting photographs along the way and sending them back to the newspaper, there's no way I could have written and filed more than two dozen stories for publication or transmitted 200 photographs during the course of the trip or corresponded with colleagues and readers through e-mail without a laptop computer, a digital camera and lots of electrical receptacles and accessible phone lines. The cell phone also made it remarkably easy to stay in touch with editors and curious grandmothers.

It was purely coincidental — and hilarious to us — that we embarked on our trip at the same time the nation was becoming obsessed with the "Survivor" television series. The newspaper produced a funny television commercial to promote our trip and used "Survivor" as a theme, comparing us to those stranded on the island. Actually, we had absolutely no connection to the

I can admire what Lewis and Clark accomplished without wishing I could have gone along for the ride.

show. However, at times we did feel as if we were stranded, and tensions occasionally did arise among the alliances. But no one was voted off the van (although some days the balloting was close).

We spent 51 days on the road and traveled nearly 10,000 miles, venturing into 28 states. It was good to be home and sleep in our own beds. But it was only a few days before we began to reminisce about our trip. We missed the daily sense of adventure — if not the driving — and the unparalleled opportunity to discover America the beautiful: wild and wonderful, tamed and tacky.

For those readers who traveled with us through our stories in the Richmond Times-Dispatch, it's nice to have you back. For new readers, we hope you enjoy the ride.

Richmond Times-Dispatch (http://www.timesdispatch.com)
Recreational Vehicle Industry Association (http://www.rvia.org)
AAA (http://www.aaamidatlantic.com)
Vanworks (http://www.vanworks.com)
Rand McNally TripMaker and StreetFinder (http://www.randmcnally.com)

We spent 51 days on the road and traveled nearly 10,000 miles, venturing into 28 states. It was good to be home and sleep in our own beds. But it was only a few days before we began to reminisce about our trip.

How we packed before setting out

ON THE ROAD — A journey of 10,000 miles begins with a single step.

Ours began with a stop at the public library. For months we've been meticulously planning this seven-week odyssey across America and the first destination on our glorious itinerary turns out to be the library, so we can drop off a sack of books — soon to be overdue — that were unearthed while we were emptying our house and filling our van.

I wonder if this is how Lewis and Clark got started?

I can't say for sure, but I bet they weren't traveling with a 6-year-old who asked after precisely 46 minutes on the trail: "Has it been an hour yet?"

No.

Our inauspicious departure had been building. The day before we left, I was so overwhelmed, facing an ever-growing list of last-minute details and a frighteningly large pile of luggage reproducing in our garage that there was only one thing I could do: wash the van's windshield.

I think this must be a guy thing.

Earlier, I had called Marlene Graham for a pep talk. I wrote about Marlene and her family a few years ago when they sold their house in Kansas, bought a fancy van and traveled the country for a year. Seven weeks does not compare to 52, but I figured she would be a good source of advice.

"I shouldn't tell you this," Marlene told me anyway, "but the first few weeks are the hardest because it takes a while to get into the swing of things. It takes a couple of weeks to get into a groove."

If this is true, we will be grooving around Montana.

QUESTION: How do you pack for a seven-week trip for a family of five?

OUR ANSWER: Not very well.

We're driving the biggest vehicle I've ever steered — a terrific conversion van with lots of space — and we've managed to stuff the thing from bow to stern.

We've packed enough clothes to outfit a small town in Nebraska. For space considerations, we've contemplated just trashing our clothes as we dirty them, rather than actually laundering them. Sort of an "Underwear Across America" theme.

"I shouldn't tell you this," Marlene told me anyway, "but the first few weeks are the hardest because it takes a while to get into the swing of things. It takes a couple of weeks to get into a groove."

We've got games and music and books. We may get saddle sores from all of the riding, but we will be thoroughly entertained.

We've got enough maps and guidebooks and background materials on our destinations to open a visitor's center.

We've packed tools (heaven help us if I actually have to use them), duct tape and a big bottle of Advil. I don't know about the duct tape, but I'm pretty sure we'll put a dent in the Advil.

Precisely two minutes after his sister Alex had inquired about the time, Jack blurted out of the blue, "Can somebody give me some money?"

I'm not sure what he intended to buy or whether he was merely planning to invest for the future. But he asked at the precise moment we were hurtling along at 65 mph and everyone was strapped tightly into their seats like astronauts going to the moon.

We planned a long drive west for our first day. Almost 500 miles. Insane, perhaps, but we wanted to cover a good deal of ground so that we have time later to linger at places down the road we've never visited.

Funny thing, the most pleasant surprise of our first day turned out to be relatively close to home.

Because we left our home in suburban Richmond later than we'd hoped, lunchtime came while we were still in Virginia. Only seconds before I sensed there would be a hunger-inspired insurrection from the rear of the van, we saw a sign for Douthat State Park and turned off Interstate 64.

Douthat, just east of Clifton Forge, was fabulous. We ate a picnic lunch, the kids played on an impressive playground, and we strolled around a shimmering lake. We spent a couple of hours there and could have stayed much longer (which, I'm certain, will become a recurring theme for this trip).

As we continued our ride, Jack counted tractors and Alex horses, while Melissa stirred those adolescent creative juices and kept track of how many McDonald's we passed. We are very proud.

Through wild and wonderful West Virginia we went, heading for our first night in Kentucky. However, we took a short side trip and intentionally strayed into Ohio — it, like the library, wasn't in our plans — chasing a dazzling sunset on a road winding along the Ohio River. It was a few minutes out of our way, but time well spent.

It was late when we reached our first stop, just outside Lexington, Ky. Jack and Alex were

As we continued our ride, Jack counted tractors and Alex horses, while Melissa stirred those adolescent creative juices and kept track of how many McDonald's we passed.

An Original WebPointers™ Interactive Internet Guide

zonked out; I carried them both to our motel room and put them to bed without the slightest resistance — a rare but much-appreciated occurrence. Five of us in one motel room (or a single tent, as will be the case later in our journey) will be a challenge this entire trip. The first night, though, went smoothly.

One night on the road down, but miles to go before we really sleep.

Douthat State Park (http://www.dcr.state.va.us/parks/douthat.htm)

Five of us in one motel room (or a single tent, as will be the case later in our journey) will be a challenge this entire trip.

Characters come alive at Kentucky Horse Park

LEXINGTON, Ky. — In many ways, it's the people you meet along the way that makes traveling worthwhile.

People such as Will Harbut.

By all accounts, Harbut was a character with a capital "C."

I say "was" because Harbut's been gone more than a half-century. We became acquainted with him through a plaque at the Kentucky Horse Park, a marvelous piece of real estate that is part working horse farm and part tourist attraction amid the undulating pastures and white fences of the bluegrass.

The plaque memorializing Harbut is next to a shrine to Man o' War, one of the most famous, most dominating horses of all time. He was a monster of a horse with an incredible 28-foot stride when he was going full-tilt. Get out in the yard and pace off 28 feet. It will boggle your mind. Man o' War is buried beneath the statue in a casket lined with his racing colors.

Harbut was Man o' War's groom and, to hear him tell it, his confidante.

Harbut went to work with Man o' War at Faraway Farm in 1930. He eventually insisted that Man o' War could understand every word he spoke. A genial man, Harbut became Man o' War's self-appointed publicist, leading visitors through the stables at Faraway, gladly sharing the horse's legend. He told Man o' War stories in an eloquent, folksy way.

"He's the mostest hoss," Harbut used to say, "what ever drew breath."

You can't make up quotes that good.

Or facts this poignant.

"He's the mostest hoss," Harbut used to say, "what ever drew breath."

Harbut died of a heart attack in 1947, after 17 years as Man o' War's best friend. Less than a month later, the horse died, too. Man o' War was aging and had health problems, but he also might have developed a bad case of a broken heart.

I already had a soft spot in my heart for the Kentucky Horse Park when we showed up on the first official stop of our cross-country adventure.

Last fall, I took Alexandra on a pilgrimage to Lexington to see our (well, *my*) favorite basketball team: the University of Kentucky Wildcats. We spent a morning at the horse park. On the way home, we realized Alex had lost her beloved blue winter cap. We couldn't remember exactly where she had misplaced it, but the horse park was one of the possibilities. I called the park the following week and spoke to a pleasant woman who left the phone and returned a few minutes later reporting she had located the hat in the lost-and-found box and would happily mail it to us.

Earlier this week, we introduced the rest of the family to this gorgeous place where lost hats go to live.

The kids stroked horses and rode ponies and got up close with a few gangly foals. We watched an Arabian horse show. We strolled through aptly named Big Barn, which is the length of a football field and a half, contains 52 spacious stalls and is one of the largest wooden horse barns in the world.

For lunch, we found a grassy spot near our van and spread a blanket for a picnic. Our cold chicken attracted a dog and his owner, Brian, a young man from Missouri who was at the park on his honeymoon. His bride had visited the park as a kid and always wanted to come back. It was a nice wedding present for them both.

We climbed aboard a wagon pulled by a pair of massive 1,800-pound Percherons named Nick and Pete.

Jack was quite pleased by the creatures, but, frankly, he was just as thrilled at the sight of the farm tractors he spotted throughout the park. He's a New Holland man, but he didn't mind the opportunity to kick the tall tires of a green Deere.

We visited the park's International Museum of the Horse, which is one of those places you could stop and linger and spend the better part of a day. Accompanied by three kids late in the afternoon, we set a Kentucky Derby-like pace to hit the high spots and get out in time to visit the gift shop before it closed. On family vacations, gift shops represent the carrot dangling at the end of a long stick. Miss one and you're likely to pay a higher price than those really expensive tacky little knick-knacks that kids gravitate to.

Kentucky may be the home of fast horses, but it's also home of the fast break. Before heading back to the motel, we drove into downtown Lexington so the rest of the family could get a look at Rupp Arena, the basketball arena where the Wildcats play. Without being able to go inside for a peek and without 23,000 screaming fans dressed in blue, it's little more than a cold, hulk of a building. But we are sentimental folk so we lined everyone up at the entrance and brought out our cameras.

Jack was quite pleased by the creatures, but, frankly, he was just as thrilled at the sight of the farm tractors he spotted through-out the park.

It was the mostest moment of a thoroughly mostest day.

Kentucky Horse Park (http://www.kyhorsepark.com/khp/hp1.html)
International Museum of the Horse (http://www.imh.org/)
Man o' War (http://www.imh.org/imh/kyhpl6b.html#xtocid1228611)
University of Kentucky Wildcats (http://www.ukathletics.com)

... we are sentimental folk so we lined everyone up at the entrance and brought out our cameras ... the mostest moment of a thoroughly mostest day.

Seeing Big Mac marks Independence Day

ST. LOUIS — Five tickets to a St. Louis Cardinals baseball game: $95.

Four redbird-on-a-bat ball caps (Robin politely declined): $48.

Jumbo hot dogs and sodas for five: $28.50.

Seats in the shade when it's 90 degrees and muggy as a steam room on the Fourth of July: priceless.

Dumb luck enabled us to sit in the shade at Busch Stadium. I bought the tickets in February and I took what was available. They just happened to be shielded from the sun by the upper deck.

But that ranked only as the second highlight of our day. The first was going onto the field before the game while Cardinals' slugger Mark McGwire and his teammates took batting practice.

I'm a Cardinals fan from my childhood when my dad convinced me the Yankees weren't the way to go. I have similarly brainwashed my children and, to some extent, my wife, who, I'm sure, deep down, simply cannot believe she traveled more than 800 miles to watch a baseball game.

In recent years, I've gotten mixed up with a ragtag group of politicians, publicists and assorted other incurable Redbirds fans who meet on occasion in Washington to discuss the plight of our favorite team. Through this group, I've become friends with Marty Hendin, who works in the Cardinals front office and who invited us for a quick tour of the ballpark — and a visit to the field — before Tuesday's game with the Reds.

We rode down an elevator and wound through a hallway within the stadium that took us near locker rooms and other inner sanctums before we saw a ray of sunshine before us. We walked toward the light and onto the field from a tunnel behind home plate.

We stood on the gravel runway that rings the playing field. The Cardinals were taking their cuts in the batting cage. Big league baseball teams play 162 games a season and pre-game practice is a daily routine bordering on drudgery that is not typically one of the more scintillating portions of attending a ballgame.

But since McGwire became a Cardinal, thousands of fans routinely show up two hours before game time to watch Big Mac take his practice swings. Many of them gather in the outfield bleachers, hoping not only to catch a glimpse of a McGwire ball leaving the yard but also, just maybe, a ball itself.

... my wife, ... I'm sure, deep down, simply cannot believe she traveled more than 800 miles to watch a baseball game.

When it was McGwire's turn, he strode into the cage and the stadium grew quiet, as if this were church and the preacher were about to speak. The Rev. Mac spoke with his lumber, effortlessly stroking probably a dozen home run balls into the far reaches of Busch Stadium.

Watching a McGwire blast from anywhere is an event; standing at ground zero when he connects is quite something else. I enjoyed it immensely. Jack and Alex eventually found their own enjoyment playing in the gravel.

The sun was merciless and there may be no hotter place than St. Louis in July (although I feel certain I will amend this thought later this month when we enter Death Valley in the California desert). We were soaked with perspiration, although we'd done nothing more than gaze in amazement while McGwire and the other Cardinals did all the work.

So, we were grateful to reach our seats. We were even more grateful when the Cardinals scored six runs in the first inning. For the game, McGwire didn't hit a home run — although he sent Reds centerfielder Ken Griffey Jr. to the wall on one long fly-out — but Jim Edmonds, a new Cardinal who might just be the league's most valuable player, sated the crowd's thirst for power by hitting two.

The Cardinals kept hitting, the Reds kept pitching poorly and the game dragged on. More than two-and-a-half hours in, we were only in the sixth inning and Alex asked, "Daddy, can baseball games last forever?"

Theoretically, yes.

The Cardinals finally won, 14-3.

After the game we walked over to Fair Saint Louis, a zoo of a Fourth of July festival beneath the Gateway Arch along the Mississippi River. We weren't in town for the first two days of the three-day affair, but the last day — July 4 itself — was really something.

I've never seen so many people in one place. My estimate is that at least several hundred million were there and I'm pretty sure most of them brushed up against me at some point during our attempt to navigate from one end to the other of the riverfront site, which is all part of the Jefferson National Expansion Memorial.

By the way, the Museum of Westward Expansion, situated underground at the base of the Arch is a terrific place to spend a couple of hours. It is interesting, informative and inspiring on a number

When it was McGwire's turn, he strode into the cage and the stadium grew quiet, as if this were church and the preacher were about to speak.

of levels that all ages can appreciate. There also are a couple of movies to catch including a breathtaking one about the construction of the Arch.

At the fair, there was lots of music, a wide range of food — we particularly enjoyed the jambalaya and homemade potato chips — and fireworks to put an exclamation point on the whole thing. We didn't make it to the fireworks; too many people and too much excitement earlier in the day. We retreated to our room at the Marriott Pavilion Hotel, which is across the street from Busch Stadium and only a few blocks from the Arch. From our 15th-floor room, we had a fine view of the fireworks — plus the kids could snuggle up in their sleeping bags, wearing the 3-D fireworks glasses and waving the miniature American flags their grandmother had sent with them.

We wrapped up our stay in St. Louis the next morning, riding the tiny tram that runs inside the Arch to the top — 630 feet from the ground. On windy days, the Arch actually sways, which, from a previous visit, I knew to be quite a thrill.

We were fortunate on two counts. It wasn't windy the day we went up. Plus, the slit-like windows that provide unparalleled views of the river and the city are sealed shut and too small for tourists like us to fall through.

St. Louis Cardinals (http://www.stlcardinals.com/)
Jefferson National Expansion Memorial (http://www.nps.gov/jeff/Default.htm)
Museum of Westward Expansion (http://www.gatewayarch.com/museum.html)
Marriott Pavilion Hotel (http://www.marriotthotels.com/stlpv/)
St. Louis Convention & Visitors Commission (http://www.explorestlouis.com)

From our 15th-floor room, we had a fine view of the fireworks — plus the kids could snuggle up in their sleeping bags, wearing the 3-D fireworks glasses and waving the miniature American flags their grandmother had sent with them.

They built it and we came

Don and Becky Lansing... own the ball field ... that was made famous in the movie "Field of Dreams." Some people found the movie hokey. I found it to be one of my favorites.

DYERSVILLE, Iowa — Is this heaven?

Our 3-year-old Jack thinks it may be.

His old man is right with him.

This is where we both found our Field of Dreams.

Jack loves tractors, and the countryside here in northeastern Iowa is crawling with them. They're part of the landscape. They're part of the traffic. They're part of the culture.

I give you the National Farm Toy Museum, two floors of more than 30,000 toy tractors, trucks and all sorts of other miniature farm equipment. It's even got a 45-seat theater. Farming, even when it involves toys, is serious business here.

Jack was absolutely mesmerized. He does not come from a family that is particularly familiar with farm machinery, but we have a friend in the tractor business and Jack has come to know and appreciate the work of hay balers, combines and backhoes. He shared his knowledge — authoritatively, I might add — with everyone within earshot at the museum. Otherwise, we fell in behind a farm family touring the place and eavesdropped on the information being dispensed by the dad, who obviously knew what he was talking about.

Later, we visited the nearby Ertl toy outlet. Ertl, based in Dyersville, is a huge worldwide company that manufactures farm toys. We saw toys we didn't even know existed.

Jack was practically drooling.

That afternoon, it was my turn to drool.

We drove a few miles outside town to the home of Don and Becky Lansing. They own the ball field (most of it, anyway) carved from cornfields that was made famous in the movie "Field of Dreams." Some people found the movie hokey. I found it to be one of my favorites.

Eleven years after the movie, the field remains stunningly beautiful. The grass lush and green. The infield dirt of crushed red brick still looks Hollywood-ready and still crunches under your feet the way it did under Shoeless Joe's. The surrounding corn is not much more than chest-high at this time of summer, but if you walk among the rows and listen closely as the wind eerily rustles the stalks, you swear you can hear the ghosts of players past.

And the numbers of tourists remain stunningly large. More than 50,000 a year, said the Lansings.

A lot of people figured the novelty of a baseball diamond in the middle of a farm in northeast Iowa would wear off after a while. A lot of people were wrong.

If you build it, they will come.

They're still coming.

"A lot of people in town said it would die out," said Don Lansing, whose family has owned the farm for more than 90 years. "But it didn't."

One of those tourists was Becky Lansing. She was a widow. On her visit in 1995, she met Don. They hit it off and were married a year later. Now, they are the proud parents of a national treasure.

"This is our child," said Becky.

It was hot the afternoon we showed up, the way it is in July in Iowa. Azure sky, pillows of clouds. Several dads were pitching to their kids. My children and I brought our gloves out of the van and had a catch, a tribute to the Kevin Costner line at the end of the movie when he asked his dad if he wanted "to have a catch." I loved that line even though while I've "played" catch and "made" a catch, I'd never actually "had" a catch. Until now.

We eventually moved to home plate where I pitched wiffle balls to Alex.

Batting is fine, but when you're that age, running the bases is the thing. So, run the bases Alex did. At one point, when Jack went to tag her with the ball, she slid into home. She was beaming when she popped up to show me blood trickling from her scraped-up leg.

While some people come to play, others simply come to sit in the tiny bleachers and soak in the aura of the place.

"There are as many different reasons people come here as there are people," said Becky. "Some come for the spirituality. A few for reconciliation. Some just for the love of baseball."

This might be a place of dreams and magic, but the real world has intruded on it.

The field straddles two farms. The moviemakers picked the spot for the field based on its proximity to the Lansings' white farmhouse. But that meant left field and part of center field belonged to the neighboring farm. After the movie was completed, the neighbor replanted his part of the field in corn. When tourists started flocking to the Lansing farm, he reversed field and cleared his again.

"There are as many different reasons people come here as there are people," said Becky. "Some come for the spirituality. A few for reconciliation. Some just for the love of baseball."

The relations between the two neighbors was cool. Now, an investment group has purchased the neighboring farm. The Lansings' part of the property is known as "Field of Dreams" Movie Site; the other is Left and Center Field of Dreams. There are two driveways — just a few feet apart — that lead visitors to the same place. There are two souvenir stands and two closing times; the Lansings shut down the infield and right field at 6 p.m., while Left and Center Field remains open until sunset.

Neither charges an admission fee, although Left and Center Field of Dreams charges $6 to walk through a maze cut into its corn.

Laughed Becky Lansing, "We remind people they are very much welcome to get chiggers and walk through our corn for free."

Don is retired from John Deere. The Lansings lease their cropland. They make enough money from the sale of souvenirs to break even on the field upkeep, which is substantial considering how immaculate it remains.

Having a tourist attraction in your backyard can be a curse sometimes, Becky said. But the feeling passes. The notion of owning something held so dear by so many — and being able to share it — makes it worthwhile.

Before we left, Becky invited us to the porch of their house, made famous in the movie. The kids sat in their porch swing. Becky took Jack around back to sit on the tractor Costner drove in the film. Jack really likes Iowa.

I wondered if Becky and Don would ever consider plowing up the ball field and replanting it in corn. I wondered this as still more visitors, arriving in vans and campers bearing license plates from all over, pulled into the Lansings' little parking lot behind home plate.

"If we did," said Becky with a laugh, "we'd have to move out of the country."

Becky took Jack around back to sit on the tractor Costner drove in the film. Jack really likes Iowa.

Field of Dreams (http://www.fieldofdreamsmoviesite.com/distance.html)
Left and Center Field of Dreams (http://www.leftandcenterfod.com/)
National Farm Toy Museum (http://www.dyersville.org/museum.htm)
Ertl Toy Outlet (http://www.ertltoys.com)

An Original *Web*Pointers™ Interactive Internet Guide

Cornhuskers celebrate chicken

WAYNE, Neb. — Del Hampton drove 600 miles to cluck like a chicken.

But he's an extremely good clucker, and the long drive to the Wayne Chicken Show proved worthwhile. He drove home to Fort Smith, Ark., with a big trophy in the back seat and an impressive title for his resume: National Cluck-Off Champion.

I don't hang around chickens much, but Hampton sure sounded to me like he belonged in a chicken coop. Some people might not consider that much of a talent, but Hampton views it as a gift.

I asked him if, you know, he practiced around the house.

Not really, he said. His real hobby is singing and he does practice that and he gets all nervous before he sings in public. He doesn't sweat a lick before he clucks, though.

"Clucking, for some reason, just comes natural," said Hampton, who's won the national title the past two years. "It's God-given ability."

Same probably can be said for the guy who scarfed down 11 1/2 hard-boiled eggs in four minutes to win that contest. I don't know for sure, though, because I didn't want to get close enough to ask him.

The Wayne Chicken Show is an annual festival that is ostensibly about chickens but mostly about having a good time. The most recent one was held on a fiercely hot Midwest Saturday, and it just so happened that our cross-country itinerary allowed us to stop in for the day. It was our good fortune.

The local arts council dreamed up the Chicken Show more than 20 years ago when its members were trying to come up with a theme for an arts-and-crafts show.

They thought an agricultural theme would be good since Wayne is in rural northeastern Nebraska. Someone suggested corn since a lot of corn is grown in the area. But someone on the committee had a last name that sounded like corn and she said not a chance. Finally, someone suggested chickens.

"That was perfect because you can make art from eggs and feathers," said Jane O'Leary, one of the founders. "From there, the meeting disintegrated into a whole lot of jokes and puns."

The little arts-and-crafts show — the council had $65 in its treasury when it began planning the

The Wayne Chicken Show is an annual festival that is ostensibly about chickens but mostly about having a good time.

first one — turned into something much bigger than its founders ever imagined.

Now, the show is about contests such as the cluck-off and egg drop (participants stand beneath a boom truck and try to catch eggs dropped from about 25 feet; lotsa luck). There is a competition to see who has the most chicken-like legs.

Chicken Bingo used to be a favorite before it was discontinued.

"They'd put a chicken in a cage and on the bottom of the cage there was a big Bingo sheet," recalled Paula Schwarten, a former member of the show's organizing committee. "Wherever it dropped..."

Wistfully, she said, "I miss that one."

There is an omelet breakfast — $1 for a cooked-to-order omelet by a Kiwanis Club member — and a lunch of grilled chicken that's known as the "Chicken Feed." Bands played. Melissa and Alex took a Bible quiz sponsored by a local church and won a couple of RC Colas. Jack touched an actual chicken.

There is even a parade with trucks gussied up to look like chickens, Shriners in miniature pickup trucks and campaigning politicians — one earnest fellow running for some statewide office shook my hand vigorously and asked me for my vote; I told him he could have it. There were fire trucks, tractors and assorted floats bearing wide-eyed young people soaking friends sitting along the curb with water rifles.

For me, the highlight of the parade was the float carrying a bunch of chunky, gyrating, shirtless guys know as "The Chickendales."

Dave Ewing, a member of the Chicken Show organizing committee, said people ask him what's required to become a Chickendale.

"About a 40-inch waist," he tells them.

The Chicken Show is held beneath towering ash and locust trees in Bressler Park in the middle of town. A neighborhood surrounds the park. Streets are closed for the Chicken Show. It seems like everyone in Wayne is either working the show or attending it. And bringing a friend.

An estimated 10,000 people — about twice Wayne's population — show up every year on the second Saturday in July. People come from Omaha and California and, yes, Virginia.

"For Wayne, it's become a major event," said O'Leary. "It's brought us a lot of attention. It's not

... one earnest fellow running for some state-wide office shook my hand vigor-ously and asked me for my vote; I told him he could have it.

only a tourist attraction, but I think people see Wayne as a creative community."

We had a fine time. Good eats, good laughs, nice people. Unpretentious, too.

Those actual chickens Jack touched were among several made available to kids for petting. Robin struck up a conversation with the woman who owns them. She and her husband live on a farm outside Wayne. Robin asked her for the name of her farm.

"We don't really have a name," she said. "We just call it our farm."

Not everyone is quite so fond of chickens. Even the people who dreamed up the Chicken Show.

"What has always been really funny is that people just assumed we did this because we really like chickens," said O'Leary, with a laugh. "I think all of us on the original committee had grown up gathering eggs on farms, but none of us had any particular appreciation for chickens.

"I can remember putting on gloves and long sleeves in the summer time so I wouldn't get pecked by some stupid chicken."

Wayne Chicken Show (http://www.chickenshow.com/)
Nebraska Division of Tourism & Travel (http://www.visitnebraska.org)

We had a fine time. Good eats, good laughs, nice people. Unpretentious, too.

Life in the conversion van is good, so far

ON THE ROAD — If it's Saturday, it must be bath night!

When you're traveling great distances in short periods of time with children, we've discovered things like nightly baths for the kids become, well, more occasional.

Almost two weeks into our cross-country vacation, we have stumbled upon other truths:

* We packed too much.

* We forgot there are only 24 hours in a day.

* Iowa sure grows a lot of corn.

* And last, and certainly least, Alex has learned to burp. (Actual quote uttered with great pride from the far back seat: "I had a *real* burp, even better than Mary Grace!" Note to Mary Grace's parents: It was a proud moment for us, too.)

We have experienced our share of family meltdowns. With kids, they are bound to occur. We wished they wouldn't, but they do. Someone's hungry. Someone doesn't like what's on the dinner menu. Someone wants to go to the gift shop. Someone doesn't want to ride any longer. Someone needs to go to the bathroom.

Everybody's tired.

We are spending a great many hours in close quarters — the conversion van is great, but it's not a two-story Colonial — and there has been occasional picking at each other.

But we go to sleep and start fresh in the morning. (Fresher some mornings than others; see reference above to baths.)

The arrangement of five of us in one room has worked out far better than I imagined.

We've given ourselves a little breathing room in the van, having relented in the middle of Iowa and packed up two boxes to ship home. They contained things we learned we don't need — bringing along materials to make scrapbooks of our trip was a fine idea, but it became clear there just wasn't going to be time to work on them — and souvenirs we've purchased. UPS is a wonderful thing.

We've had good fortune with our lodging, even in places we didn't have reservations. We've stayed primarily in basic motels. The kids alternate sleeping in the second bed in the room or bunking down in their sleeping bags. The arrangement of five of us in one room has worked out far better than I imagined.

An Original *WebPointers*™ Interactive Internet Guide

The drive itself has been enjoyable and relatively uneventful with one notable exception. The leg from St. Louis to Dyersville, Iowa, was almost a killer.

After riding up into the Gateway Arch on our getaway morning, we left St. Louis later than we'd hoped. A cranky child slowed us down further. Bad traffic ground us to a halt. Let's have a picnic! Which is precisely what we did.

It was 2:30 p.m. before we left St. Louis. We drove the river road along the Mississippi to Hannibal, Mo., the boyhood home of Mark Twain. However, we arrived just as most everything was closing. We walked around town a while and decided to stay for dinner. At about the same time, Jack decided he needed to use the bathroom *really* bad.

We had narrowed our choices for dinner to Becky Thatcher's Restaurant or Mark Twain's Family Restaurant. But when Jack announced his requirements, we were standing in front of a Subway, which had restrooms in the back. I ordered a chicken-salad sub.

We learned fireworks were scheduled for 9 p.m. — this was July 5, so these were bonus fireworks — over the Mississippi. Sounded good. We were already behind schedule. What's a couple of more hours? Dyersville was 250 miles away, but I figured the kids could sleep and I could drive. No sweat.

Sweat.

While we waited for the fireworks, I got out my laptop computer and wrote a story literally sitting on the banks of the Mississippi. We enjoyed the fireworks. Huck and Tom would have liked the noise. In fact, it might have been those two who set off the firecracker in the women's bathroom at the riverfront park just before the official fun began.

After the fireworks and the ensuing traffic jam in Hannibal, we finally headed north.

Around the Iowa border, we encountered fog. Thick fog. Fog like pudding. The road varied between four lanes and two. At least, I thought it did. In spots, I couldn't see much farther than the hood of the van. This was probably not the smartest move I'll make on this trip, but I kept going. We really wanted to get to Dyersville, home of the "Field of Dreams" ball field and the National Farm Toy Museum, so we could have more time there. The kids were asleep. I kept driving slower, hunched over the steering wheel, fearing every set of headlights I saw coming at me.

It was extremely stupid to continue. But we did.

Somehow we made it safely. Maybe it was the medal of St. Christopher — the Catholic patron

Thick fog. Fog like pudding. The road varied between four lanes and two. At least, I thought it did. In spots, I couldn't see much farther than the hood of the van.

saint of travelers — that I clipped to the visor. A friend had given it to us before we left home. We're Presbyterian but not proud.

Finally, we made it to Dyersville, where the fog seemed thickest. It was 3:30 a.m. We had no lodging reservation for that night, but we had one for the next so I headed to that motel, even though I had no real clue where it was. I crawled off the highway exit ramp. Mercy shined on us even if the moon couldn't; the only lighted sign I saw when I got off the ramp was the one for our motel. Unfortunately, the office was closed and I couldn't roust the resident-manager.

We parked in the motel lot. Robin and I reclined our seats and slept for a while. A very short while. At 4, we were awakened by a gnat who, in the deathly quiet of the van, sounded very much like a 747. At 4:30, Jack awakened us with more requirements; he watered a tree. At 6:30, I awoke and returned to the motel office. The manager, up then, was most gracious and allowed us to check in early for the next night. So, we'd essentially slept in the van and saved the cost of a night's lodging, but we didn't feel much like celebrating. Just sleeping.

But that's been the roughest part of the trip. The people we've met along the way have been exceedingly nice, such as the women working at an Indiana visitors center. I asked one if she could suggest a nearby spot for a picnic lunch, and she steered us to a wonderful playground where she took her children when they were younger. Another woman noticed Robin admiring the pretty hibiscus plants outside the center and offered her hibiscus seeds from her mother's garden.

Driving into Iowa was brutal, but the drive west across the state a couple of days later was beautiful. Corn fields as far as the eye can see, interrupted only, it seemed, by small towns, brightly illuminated country baseball diamonds, and an occasional Dairy Queen.

Nebraska and South Dakota featured fewer crops and more open pastures, but the prairie is beautiful in its way — except for maybe the incredible number of kamikaze bugs splattering against our windshield on I-90 through South Dakota. Alex has been asking since February when we would see the plains, which she had read about in school. We told her to take a good look.

We snapped all sorts of photographs from the side of the road. I'm sure when we get home and start going through our pictures we will wonder why we have so many wide-angle shots of grass.

It's been great fun so far. In addition to our primary destinations, we've managed to sneak in a few side trips to other places, such as Abraham Lincoln's boyhood farm in southern Indiana and the Corn Palace in Mitchell, S.D., a marvelous old structure featuring murals composed of locally grown

I crawled off the highway exit ramp. Mercy shined on us even if the moon couldn't; the only lighted sign I saw when I got off the ramp was the one for our motel.

34

corn and grains. The Corn Palace serves as an auditorium, basketball arena and huge source of community pride.

Gas prices haven't been particularly bad. The highest we've paid is $1.74 for premium unleaded in South Dakota.

Less than a third of the way into this trip, our bigger problems are the twin enemies of time and a budding case of homesickness.

The lack of time to explore everything is frustrating but manageable; the homesickness could be more difficult to handle. Particularly when a 3-year-old tells you, "I'm thinking about my toys, and I'm thinking about my bed."

Hannibal, MO (http://hanmo.com/jcs/)
Abraham Lincoln's Boyhood Farm (http://www.nps.gov/libo)
Corn Palace (http://www.cornpalace.org/cornpalace.html)

Less than a third of the way into this trip, our bigger problems are the twin enemies of time and a budding case of homesickness.

Free ice water draws crowds to Wall

WALL, S.D. — Out here in the middle of nowhere, the weirdly beautiful Badlands might be only the second most unlikely thing to rise up from the Great Plains.

The most unlikely? How about Wall Drug Store?

From a tiny, struggling little pharmacy in the Depression, Wall Drug has exploded on the prairie into a major tourist waystation and a world-famous American original.

Its secret to success? Free ice water.

Only in America.

"To me, it's pretty amazing," said Gayle Eisenbraun, who grew up in Connecticut, met and married a South Dakota boy, and moved here 30 years ago. She's worked at Wall Drug for 29 years.

It's amazing to a lot of people.

In 1931, Ted Hustead, a pharmacist, and his wife Dorothy came to Wall and bought the little Wall Drug Store on Main Street. Friends and relatives thought he was crazy. Early on, their view seemed prophetic.

Wall was a small town on the edge of the Badlands, the spectacularly odd landscape that some have compared to a moonscape. Few people lived there and fewer still stopped by for a visit.

Hustead gave himself five years to make a go of it. He was well into the fifth year and wasn't making much of a go of it at all. One hot summer afternoon, Dorothy left the store and took the two children to their rented room on the outskirts of town for a nap. She returned a short while later with an idea.

Friends and relatives thought he was crazy. Early on, their view seemed prophetic.

The noise of the cars passing by on the nearby highway had prevented the kids from sleeping, but it also had made Dorothy think of a way to get the people to stop at Wall Drug. She figured those travelers were bound to be thirsty and there wasn't much good drinking water in the middle of South Dakota in those days. Her suggestion: offer them free ice water.

Bingo!

The Husteads put up Burma Shave-like billboards along the highway. A monster of a business was born.

36

"Get a soda

Get a root beer

Turn next corner

Just as near

To Highway 16 and 14

Free ice water

Wall Drug"

It wasn't exactly Longfellow, but people started coming — the opening of Mount Rushmore 60 miles away in the 1940s certainly helped — and they haven't stopped. Not only did they come, but they took away Wall Drug bumper stickers and signs, posting them all over the world to let folks know how far a drive they had to get free ice water. There's a sign in Antarctica. A native South Dakotan astronaut plastered one aboard a space shuttle. Nothing like free advertising to promote free ice water.

Wall Drug is far, far more extensive than back when Ted Hustead used to cut winter ice from nearby farm ponds and store it for summer. Wall Drug now covers about 70,000 square feet and takes up most of a block on Wall's Main Street. But the ice water is still free and the coffee is still a nickel.

It also is still a drug store, although not too many people come in to get their prescriptions filled anymore.

Now, Wall Drug is souvenir and clothing stores, restaurants and art galleries. There's even a pretty little chapel tucked between the stores; Ted Hustead was a devout Catholic who chose Wall as a place to live, in part, because there was a Catholic church in town where he could attend services every day.

There's a little bit of everything for just about everybody. You can buy a buffalo burger and high-quality jewelry, a cowboy's leather gun holster and, for $4.98, a Frisbee-like throwing disc that looks like a buffalo chip. A Chip Chucker, it's called.

Goofy is good at Wall Drug. Ted had the courage to start the store, but it was his son Bill who turned it into an attraction. Bill was an avid collector of original Western art and historical photographs that he put on display. But he also installed the life-size, animated Cowboy Orchestra and Chuckwagon Quartet. There are statues of Indian chiefs and Buffalo Bill to pose with.

Goofy is good at Wall Drug. Ted had the courage to start the store, but it was his son Bill who turned it into an attraction.

In the store's "backyard," children can climb on a giant jack-a-lope, a phony half-jackrabbit, half antelope creature whose mythical existence Wall Drug happily helps perpetuate. And every 12 minutes, with lights flashing and smoke billowing, a huge, mechanical tyrannosaurus rex rises up and snorts and roars for no apparent reason other than good-natured, over-the-top silliness.

"Some people think it's a little kitschy and think we should get rid of it, but I think that would be a big mistake," said Teddy Hustead, president of Wall Drug and grandson of the founder, as we stood on Main Street in front of his store. "I think that's part of the soul of Wall Drug."

Melissa, Alex and Jack thought this was all just swell. Robin kept thinking we should be in the Black Hills. I thought it was a good story.

Wall Drug is attracting third-generation customers these days, which is only right since the store has been passed down to a third generation of Husteads. Ted and Bill Hustead died last year — Ted at age 96, Bill at 72 of Lou Gehrig's Disease — and now Teddy and his brother Rick, who is chairman of the board, run the show.

"It's just a really good place to raise children," said Eisenbraun, who has three sons. "You can't beat a small town for neighbors. Everybody pitches in to help each other."

Wall remains a small town. It has four churches, a couple of bars, a Dairy queen and three gas stations. It has 830 permanent residents, but on a busy summer day at Wall Drug, the population can swell to 20,830.

Gayle Eisenbraun, Hustead's executive secretary, gave me the nickel tour, which her boss said some local people believe is worth at least 50 cents. Eisenbraun said she wasn't all that crazy about Wall when she first arrived. Her father told her it was "no man's land."

The Badlands can be brutally hot in the summer and wretched in the winter. But the place has grown on her. Wall — and Wall Drug — is her home.

"It's just a really good place to raise children," said Eisenbraun, who has three sons. "You can't beat a small town for neighbors. Everybody pitches in to help each other."

As an added bonus, she said with a laugh, "You can see storms coming for quite a ways."

As well as tourists.

Wall Drug (http://www.walldrug.com)
Wall, SD (http://www.wall-badlands.com/)
Mount Rushmore National Memorial (http://www.nps.gov/moru)
South Dakota Department of Tourism (http://www.travelsd.com)

Cowboys/girls impressed us tenderfoots

CODY, Wyo. — Midway through the Cody Rodeo, the public address announcer invited all the kids to come down into the arena to chase a calf and try to grab the ribbons tied to its tail.

Dozens of kids accepted the invitation and streamed out of the grandstand to form a small mob on the rodeo dirt. Melissa wasn't interested and Jack was too young. Neither budged. But Alex, who seems willing to try most anything once, got wide-eyed and wiggly.

Robin and I told her to forget it.

I guess we're just not cow-chasing people.

It became clear just how tender our feet are long before we arrived at the rodeo. This is beautiful but tough country.

We began our trip across Wyoming on a dirt road, a detour around highway construction on our way to Devils Tower National Monument in the northeast corner of the state. We wanted to take back roads during our cross-country adventure. Be careful what you wish for.

Devils Tower is a geological marvel, a gigantic stump-like formation that provides a hint of the handsome but rugged terrain that awaited pioneers in the late 1800s — and us just a few days ago.

A fellow we met in Nebraska told us the prairie — *his* prairie — can be a pretty empty, wide-open place. But Wyoming, he said, is "really desolate."

He wasn't kidding.

After we left the dirt road and hopped on Interstate 90 across Wyoming, then smaller roads winding through the Bighorn Mountains, we would drive miles without seeing a town or a soul. Flat, then mountainous, then flat again. The scenery was lovely, the colors vibrant. It's the one thing you notice right off about the Big Sky of the West: the sky is bluer, the clouds whiter, the hills a glorious gold.

The land was pretty but harsh and dry. The lush farms of the Midwest had given way to ranches with no crops and only occasional livestock visible from the highway. Robin was struck by how lonely it appeared.

This is how it seemed to us in the year 2000, traveling in an air-conditioned machine with cupholders. I can't imagine the impression this place must have left on someone bouncing along in a Conestoga wagon.

Alex, who seems willing to try most any-thing once, got wide-eyed and wiggly.

My admiration is high for those who went before us.

We eventually reached Cody, our gateway to Yellowstone National Park — and most everyone else's it seemed. After miles of nothing and no one, Cody was an honest-to-goodness tourist town. And one thing tourists do in Cody in the summer is attend the nightly rodeo.

We appreciated the skills of the cowboys and cowgirls and realized most rodeo stunts derive from actual ranch work, but it wasn't our glass of iced tea. The kids especially were put off by cowboys roping calves and tying up their legs.

"They're being mean to the baby cows," analyzed Jack.

Nothing personal, but we found ourselves rooting for the animals.

We did enjoy the plain ol' horse-riding competition, which involved skill and finesse as riders and their horses negotiated sharp turns around barrels but no one wrestling anything to the ground.

We also enjoyed watching the woman sitting a couple of rows in front of us. She was a local who seemed to know many of the competitors and certainly knew her rodeo. She was genuinely enthusiastic, hooting and hollering for every cowboy and cowgirl. If rodeo is an acquired taste, she's got it, while we've got some acquiring to do.

But there was no such cultural divide the next day when we visited the Buffalo Bill Historical Center, a wonderful repository of Western art and artifacts. It's truly a tribute to the West, representing the mythic as well as the factual, sort of like its namesake. The Center includes the Buffalo Bill Museum, the Whitney Gallery of Western Art, the Plains Indian Museum, and the Cody Firearms Museum.

Short of time, we spent only two hours there. We could have spent two days. Strolling through and eyeballing the saddles and paintings and pieces of every-day life, you really get a feel for the West.

Despite the museums' extensive and varied collections, the kids were restless and disagreeable. Too many long drives and late nights, I guess. But Joy Christensen got their attention.

Christensen, dressed in western garb and wearing her braided pony tail almost to her knees, was at the museum to talk about growing up in the West. A real, live cowgirl.

She demonstrated roping techniques and played the harmonica. Jack, a blues man in the making, loves the harmonica and he quickly took a seat as Christensen played a variety of songs on a

"They're being mean to the baby cows," analyzed Jack.

Nothing personal, but we found ourselves rooting for the animals.

variety of harmonicas. She then gave him — and Robin — a music lesson.

Turns out Christensen was born in Montana but lived all over the West, as her family traveled from one ranch to another, wherever they could find work. They had no radio or phonograph, so she learned to play the harmonica and provide the family's entertainment. She attended one-room country schools and not only saw the work on a ranch but did it. She knows what she's talking about.

She's a grandmother now with a lifetime of perspective and appreciation for the experience.

"It was a hard life, but you look back and say, 'Gosh, I was blessed!'" said Christensen. "Even if you didn't think so at the time."

Our journey continued that afternoon with a relatively short jaunt — for this trip — to Yellowstone. It was only about 50 miles through Wapiti Valley, but it was some drive. Teddy Roosevelt called it "the most scenic 50 miles in America." You can take him at his word.

We took our time. I was in no real hurry. I was eager to see Yellowstone, but I was somewhat less excited about the four nights of camping that awaited us. Two adults, three kids, hundreds of grizzly bears and one, measly little tent.

Heaven help us.

Cody Rodeo (http://www.codystampederodeo.org/)
Devils Tower National Monument (http://www.nps.gov/deto/home.htm)
Buffalo Bill Historical Center (http://www.bbhc.org)
Buffalo Bill Museum (http://www.bbhc.org/bbm_firstpage.html)
Whitney Gallery of Western Art (http://www.bbhc.org/wgwa_firstpage.html)
Plains Indian Museum (http://www.bbhc.org/pim_reinstallation.html)
Cody Firearms Museum (http://www.bbhc.org/cfm_firstpage.html)

"It was a hard life, but you look back and say, 'Gosh, I was blessed!'" said Christensen. "Even if you didn't think so at the time."

Bearing up well in Yellowstone's wilds

YELLOWSTONE NATIONAL PARK, Wyo. — It was midnight and the five of us were snug in our sleeping bags, zipped shut in our cozy tent, lined up in a row like weenies on a grill.

Except someone turned off the grill.

The temperature had plummeted to near 40 degrees, frightfully cold for Virginians in July but just right for Yellowstone, the granddaddy of America's national parks.

Camping is not my bag, so to speak. I've slept out of doors in a tent only once before — and that was at Maymont, a small city park, where the animals were behind walls and glass.

Out here in the true wilderness, you're in the animals' backyard. You get the feeling a bear will hold the door for you at the campground's public restroom.

Bears are everywhere in Yellowstone. The only thing more prevalent than bears in Yellowstone are warnings about bears in Yellowstone. There are strict rules and regulations about food and trash and where you can store your toothpaste.

Still, we did not see a single bear during our stay. We saw elk, mule deer and lots of bison. But no bear. I'm just as glad. I consider it adventurous enough to sleep in the same county with bears. I don't need to see them. I'm pleased to take the rangers' word for them.

But back to camping.

This was the portion of our cross-country trek I feared the most. I was not excited about sleeping with the animals or standing in line to take a shower or hearing other people snore. When I think of fun, camping does not emerge in my Top 10.

Well, after four days in the woods, I can say this: we lived.

Not well. But we lived.

The tent went up perfectly. Only hitch was that in all of the stuff we crammed into the conversion van, our second air mattress was nowhere to be found. It's somewhere in our house in Richmond doing no one any good at all. The first night, we tried sleeping with 2 1/2 of us on the one mattress and the rest of us on the ground. Alex woke up with condensation on her and her sleeping buddy, a stuffed dog named Mudge. We bought an air mattress at the local camp store the next day.

I don't know whether the lack of an air mattress caused our middle child to be covered in dew,

Bears are everywhere in Yellowstone. The only thing more prevalent than bears in Yellowstone are warnings about bears in Yellowstone.

An Original *WebPointers*™ Interactive Internet Guide

but I know it had nothing to do with our youngest, Jack, grinding his teeth in his sleep. He does that anyway, a nice little trait I passed on to him. Usually, it's not a big problem since he does it in his own room at home. Here, though, we're all within inches of each other. After a night of Jack crunching his teeth and slapping his gums, Robin, who had the pleasure of sleeping next to her baby, renamed him, Chompy the Goat.

Chompy woke up after that first night and announced: "I liked it better when we camped in a hotel."

And the bathing. I've been sworn not to disclose how long we went without a formal bath, but I can tell you the sun came up several times between showers. We went into a store in Grand Teton National Park, just south of Yellowstone, and the kindly woman at the counter commented to Robin that she had "some beautiful children."

Robin thought — and relayed to me a few minutes later — "It's a good thing she couldn't smell them."

I must say, though, camping wound up not being so bad.

I'd worried about how well the kids would settle down in the evenings. That really wasn't an issue. We stayed so busy seeing and doing things during the day that by dinnertime they were hungry and by bedtime (which wound up being much later than normal) they were worn out. So, they ate and slept. As a parent, you can't ask for much more.

We cooked — not extravagantly, but we cooked — on our two-burner camp stove.

Actual conversation: "What's for dinner?"

"Pick a can."

We built camp fires and made s'mores. We slept adequately, if not particularly comfortably. We grew closer as a family; three of us actually are attached now. (I'm kidding.)

Mostly, though, we saw Yellowstone and Grand Teton, nice payoffs for sleeping in a tent.

These places are nature's amusement parks. Yellowstone has rivers and lakes and meadows and waterfalls and peaks and canyons and geysers and steaming thermal pools the color of the deepest blue you can imagine. It also has nasty scars from the 1988 fires that burned more than one-third of the park. Wide stands of bare, dead trees still cover many mountainsides. New growth is slowly emerging. It's a natural process and Yellowstone will be stunning once again, but it makes you ache a little to know how beautiful it must have been.

I've been sworn not to disclose how long we went without a formal bath, but I can tell you the sun came up several times between showers.

Grand Teton is more of a postcard with its clear lakes butting up against tall, snow-capped peaks. Absolutely gorgeous.

The kids will probably remember the night sky; at 7,000 feet, the sky is so big and the stars so bright you feel like you can reach up and take a drink from the Big Dipper. They also probably will recall picking up the horn of a bighorn sheep at a ranger station. Fifteen pounds that baby weighed. I got a crick in my neck just thinking about it.

Alex will remember losing her second front tooth— she can now officially request two front teeth for Christmas — in the scrambled eggs at Yellowstone's Grant Village campground. Melissa will recall fetching our water from an outdoor spigot.

Both girls will never forget the projects they did and the facts they learned to become Junior Rangers. At the ranger station where Melissa received her badge, the ranger announced to all of the other visitors that Melissa was Yellowstone's newest ranger. They applauded. I thought Melissa was going to throw up.

But what the kids will probably remember most about Yellowstone and Grand Teton are the lunches. And it won't be the peanut butter and jelly that will trigger the warm memories.

After watching Old Faithful erupt one morning in Yellowstone, we drove to nearby Biscuit Basin to see more geysers and hot pools. We parked next to the Firehole River, a quick-moving, narrow body of chilly water. We spread a blanket and ate lunch. Other people were wading, so we did, too. It was a fine time, exceeded only by the next day when we ventured down to Grand Teton and picnicked next to Jackson Lake. We pulled out the swimsuits this time and swam in the shadow of a mountain still covered with snow. The sun was hot, the water was cold, the setting was perfect. It was like splashing around in a painting.

After a couple of hours of this, Alex spread her Tigger blanket on the rocky beach, reclined and said, "No more complaining. This is the life!"

It truly was almost perfect. The only thing missing was a bar of soap.

Maymont Park (http://www.maymont.org)
Yellowstone National Park (http://www.nps.gov/yell/home.htm)
Grand Teton National Park (http://www.grand.teton.national-park.com)

The kids will probably remember the night sky; at 7,000 feet, the sky is so big and the stars so bright you feel like you can reach up and take a drink from the Big Dipper.

Monumental cleanup in Montana

ST. MARY, Mont. — Spectacular.

Absolutely spectacular.

I've never seen anything like it. The peaks, the valleys, the way it went on as far as the eye could see.

Glacier National Park? Sure, that's nice. But I'm talking about our laundry.

After more than two weeks on the road, we reached the point where one day Jack's sock selection was down to one hot pink one and one white one. The pink one wasn't his. And the white one wasn't particularly clean.

We either had to wash our dirty clothes or burn them. After a close family vote, we settled on the former.

We didn't know how to pack for a seven-week trip, but we knew we didn't want to do laundry every few days. We decided to bring all the shorts and T-shirts we could stuff into the van, as well as a token supply of cold-weather clothes.

That was a fine theory until just about every article of clothing we brought was soiled and nearly capable of standing on its own and hiking with us.

So, when we reached Glacier National Park in northern Montana, we gazed at wildflowers, stood in awe of the snow-capped peaks and washed load after load of clothes at our campground's laundry. Melissa kept the washers and dryers humming; Robin did the folding. Jack and Alex slept. I tried to look busy typing on the laptop computer.

At the end of the evening, our little rustic cabin — four walls, two windows, one door, no plumbing — looked like the scene of some horrible textile accident. Clothes were everywhere. They were clean, but they were everywhere.

More than 3,000 miles into our stair-step journey across the western United States, we were ready for another couple of weeks of clean travel.

Which we started in Glacier, one of the most breathtakingly beautiful places in the country.

Glacier is on the Canadian border and is part of the Waterton-Glacier International Peace Park. Waterton Lakes National Park is its Canadian counterpart.

So, when we reached Glacier National Park in northern Montana, we gazed at wildflowers, stood in awe of the snow-capped peaks and washed load after load of clothes at our campground's laundry.

Glacier's peaks and lakes and dramatic sheer cliffs were shaped and whittled thousands of years ago by Ice Age glaciers. Today, the park still contains numerous glaciers that feed its cold, turquoise lakes. Summer days are generally pleasant and temperatures routinely dip into the 30s on summer nights. Snowfall on July 4 temporarily shut down the park's famous Going-to-the-Sun Road.

We stayed in a commercial campground on the eastern side of Glacier in St. Mary, a small crossroads on the Blackfeet Indian Reservation. The eastern is the drier, more rugged side of the park, typically receiving less rain than the lush, green western side. But the eastern side is also the gateway to the Canadian park, which is where we spent our first day.

It was our first trip into a foreign country, although Canada didn't seem particularly foreign. The friendly customs officer asked us a few questions about our intentions (all honorable, I told her). We produced all five of our birth certificates, and no one in the van required a rabies shot, so we were passed through in short order.

We drove past the lovely Prince of Wales Hotel, which sits on a bluff above Waterton Lake and looks like a storybook castle. Even if you don't stay at the somewhat pricey hotel, you can enjoy High Tea and a heart-pounding view every afternoon. However, we weren't traveling with a High Tea crowd.

Here is a common conflict with children. While adults are happy to soak in the atmosphere, children are far less patient. That's become obvious during our trip. I took Alex on a short hike one day. She asked why we were going where we were going.

"Because it's pretty," I told her.

We got there. We looked. Ten seconds later, Alex was ready to roll.

"We've seen the prettiness," she said. "Can we go now?"

So, we've tried to sprinkle our sight-seeing with activities the kids enjoy. In Waterton, that proved to be a picnic lunch on the shore of Cameron Lake followed by an excursion on the lake aboard a pedal boat. The five of us pedaled around Cameron for an hour, eyeing the shoreline in vain for bears, and ended our visit with ice cream bars.

Our second day, we ventured into Glacier itself and took an official tour of St. Mary Lake aboard the Little Chief, a boat built in 1925 and operated by the Glacier Park Boat Co. On shore, a naturalist guided our group on a 1 1/2-mile, uphill hike to see St. Mary Falls. I'm sure glad we

"We've seen the prettiness," she said. "Can we go now?"

purchased Jack hiking shoes before the trip; they looked good on his feet, which were draped over my shoulders for most of the hike. He had a good ride.

The adventuresome part of the hike came when the naturalist stopped and gathered us around a tree whose bark, she said, had been scraped and rubbed off by bears. I'm thinking, if this is a bear's version of a favorite chair, maybe we should move along. Quickly.

Quickly, however, is not the way to travel Going-to-the-Sun, a soaring, twisting, treacherous two-lane road that provides utterly gorgeous views — for everyone other than those who are driving. Going-to-the-Sun is a 50-mile stretch of highway, carved into mountainsides, that spans the park from east to west and makes you feel at times that you're going to you-know-where. It opened in 1932, taking eight years to build, which is only slightly less time than it takes to find a parking space on July mornings at the Logan Pass visitor center, a popular stop atop the Continental Divide.

We began a 3-mile hike to Hidden Lake behind the visitor center, but had to turn back. The snow was too deep. Melting snow and slush covered the trail and made negotiating it too tricky for us. That and the fact that if you fell you would likely slide off the mountain and fall several thousand feet. (We have established "no-stitches" and "no-bone-breakage" rules for our trip.)

Still, the kids enjoyed making snowballs in July. It was Jack's biggest day since the National Farm Toy Museum in Iowa. It was good for us too; between the snow and the blooming alpine meadows, it looked like a scene from "The Sound of Music."

Once again, we were shut out on the bear watch. Glacier is home to several hundred grizzly bears and even more black bears. We heard lots of warnings but saw no bears. Just as well. We did see bighorn sheep and mountain goats and a number of guys who felt the need to traipse through the snow at Logan Pass without their shirts.

Maybe their clothes were dirty.

Waterton-Glacier International Peace Park (http://www.americanparknetwork.com/parkinfo/gl/index.html)
Blackfeet Indian Reservation (http://www.blackfeetnation.com)
Prince of Wales Hotel (http://www.fortsaskinfo.com/photos13.htm)
Going-to-the-Sun Road (http://glacier.visitmt.com/sunpr.htm)
Glacier Park Boat Co. (http://www.digisys.net/gpboats/welcome.htm)

I'm sure glad we purchased Jack hiking shoes before the trip; they looked good on his feet, which were draped over my shoulders for most of the hike.

Idaho's special people won our hearts

SANDPOINT, Idaho — Cancel the rest of the trip. We're staying in Idaho.

Not really. But the thought crossed our minds.

Every place we've visited on this cross-country journey has left us wishing for a longer stay. But Idaho was special.

Maybe it was the fabulous cabin where we bunked down at the Western Pleasure Guest Ranch, the first place we've all had beds to sleep in (as well as an actual kitchen) since we left home.

Or maybe it was the horses we rode and admired, or Star the border collie who perfectly trained our children in the fine art of playing fetch, or the barn kittens the kids chased, hugged and cuddled — and whom Jack serenaded with his harmonica — for the better part of two days.

Probably, though, it was the people: everyone from Roley and Janice Schoonover, who operate the ranch that was settled by Janice's grandparents more than 60 years ago, to the family and friends who help them run the place. That would include ranch hand Brad Yunek who cheerfully let us tag along on his various chores and told us some great stories on the way.

Yunek has roots in the Midwest, grew up mostly in Southern California, but dearly loves life here in what John Steinbeck called "the upraised thumb" of northern Idaho. This is a land of mountains and evergreens, of pleasant summers and magnificent winters. And of people who don't mind breaking a sweat.

People such as Yunek.

"It's good, clean, honest work," said Yunek of his job at the ranch. He seems right at home doctoring ailing foals or edifying gawking Easterners. He also plays a mean guitar and can sing.

I learned about the Schoonovers' ranch quite by accident. We were in need of something to do between Glacier National Park in northern Montana and the Oregon coast. Scouting around Idaho tourism sites on the World Wide Web in the spring, I came across the Western Pleasure Guest Ranch and made a few inquiries. I believe this is called serendipity.

The guest ranch business is relatively new to the Schoonovers, although the land is not. This is where Janice grew up. Janice's Grandpa Wood came here in 1940, and, along with others, was seduced by this beautiful, tempting land surrounded by the Cabinet and Selkirk mountains. He and others purchased property that had been cut by logging companies and then abandoned. "Stump

Scouting around Idaho tourism sites on the World Wide Web in the spring, I came across the Western Pleasure Guest Ranch and made a few inquiries.

48

ranches," much of the land was called. It took more than hopes and dreams to clear it and make it something worth owning.

Over the years, Janice's family purchased other land in the area for cattle ranching and other endeavors.

As time went by, though, the original ranch became expendable and the barns and other buildings fell into disrepair. For a while, the place was for sale.

Janice is grateful no one bought it. She and Roley, high school sweethearts who married while they were still teenagers, began making plans for the guest ranch in 1990. They started by guiding trail rides around their 960 acres. Once it became clear they'd hit on something, they added three log cabins tucked among the trees and, in 1996, a centerpiece: a stunning 10,000-square-foot lodge. Roley quit his day job working in the business office at a local electronics plant, and the Schoonovers and their children, Danielle, 11, and Isaac, 9, became full-time hosts.

The ranch, which the family very nearly had to sell, now appears safe.

"The whole desire was to keep the ranch in the family and this seemed like a really good way to preserve it for the next generations," said Janice.

Horseback riding is the main recreation offered at the ranch in the summer (in winter, it's horse-drawn sleigh rides and cross-country skiing). That was perfect for us. Alex loves horses and, as the Iowa tractor museum was for Jack, this stop was largely for her.

It ended up being great for all of us.

Alex, Melissa and I — the good, the bad and the ugly, although I'll never divulge who was who — took a two-hour trail ride guided by one of Janice and Roley's nieces; numerous family members help out at the ranch, including Janice's sister-in-law Naomi who does much of the cooking.

Alex and Melissa seemed to do just fine with their horses. My horse, Chisholm, a chestnut-colored quarterhorse, seemed to think we were on a dinner date. It did not pass a tree, plant or blade of grass it did not want to sample.

Occasionally, Chisholm seemed to enjoy complicating matters further by breaking into a trot, which, to my amateurish senses, felt like I was on the home stretch of the Kentucky Derby. By the end of the ride, I'd learned to say "Whoa!" instead of "Hold it!"

In general, the ride was beautiful and enjoyable, as well as revelatory, in that I discovered leg muscles I never knew I had. I hope to be walking straight again by Arizona.

In general, the ride was beautiful and enjoyable, as well as revelatory, in that I discovered leg muscles I never knew I had. I hope to be walking straight again by Arizona.

Later, we rode with Yunek aboard a four-wheeler to fetch the ranch's two veteran draft horses, Amos and Andy ("Andrew" when he misbehaves, which isn't often, Yunek said). Then we watched as Yunek harnessed the two massive Percherons and hitched them to a wagon.

One evening a week during the summer, the Schoonovers offer a chuckwagon dinner show. We hit the right night. The kids hopped aboard the wagon for a spin, and, after dinner, we sat in the lodge and listened to The Palmer Family, a quick-fingered, quick-witted, father-and-kids quartet that plays country and cowboy music. They originally are from Massachusetts, of all places, but they call Sandpoint home these days.

Our souvenirs from north Idaho include the Palmers' latest compact disc — and, of course, the sore leg muscles and a head full of sights and sounds and memories featuring critters and scenery that would not quit.

I asked Janice if it's amusing to her that city slickers can be so highly entertained by things that must be humdrum to her.

Not at all, she said. For the few years she lived in nearby Washington state when Roley was in college, she desperately missed home and knew the Idaho ranch was where she belonged.

"The little things kind of entertain me, too," she said. "Sometimes I enjoy it more than the guests.

"I hope I never get to the point where I take this stuff for granted."

We will miss the big breakfasts in the lodge, staying in a place where the doors are never locked, and the sense of humor of everyone we met.

"You know the ranch rules," Roley said with a straight face when it was brought to his attention that the kids were infatuated with the kittens. "You touch one, you take it."

I'm pretty sure he was kidding, but we did a kitty check in the back of the van before pulling away, just to make sure.

Western Pleasure Guest Ranch (http://www.westernpleasureranch.com/)
Idaho Travel and Tourism (http://www.visitid.org)
Palmer Family (http://www.proaxis.com/~joes/palmer/index.htm)

We will miss the big breakfasts in the lodge, staying in a place where the doors are never locked, and the sense of humor of everyone we met.

Late picnic visitors turn out to be wallaroos

DALLESPORT, Wa. — Our late picnic lunch was over and we were wadding up our paper plates, throwing.out the remnants of our peanut-butter-and-jelly sandwiches and shaking out our blanket.

It was 4 o'clock on a sunny afternoon and the grassy, hillside park in Spokane — which we literally had stumbled on just as we were about to return to the interstate highway — was deserted except for us.

Then a man showed up with a couple of backpacks. He sat down, opened his backpacks, pulled out two cloth pouches — and out scrambled two kangaroos.

I kid you not.

Except they weren't kangaroos. They were wallaroos — sort of like wallabees, but more sociable, said the man with the backpacks, John Schreiner Jr.

Turns out Schreiner is president of a real estate title company in Spokane, in far eastern Washington. It also turns out he owns a 12,000-acre ranch where he and his brother raise exotic animals such as zebras, yaks and wallaroos.

It further turns out that his ranch, Schreiner Farms, is almost 300 miles from Spokane in the Columbia River town of Dallesport, which was precisely the area we were heading when we encountered Schreiner.

He gave us the name and number of his ranch foreman — he even took my notebook and scribbled down specific driving directions as well as a motel recommendation — and told us he would call ahead and arrange a tour of the place for us.

We spent the night in The Dalles, Ore., just across the mighty Columbia from Dallesport. Next morning, we showed up at the ranch, not knowing for sure if Schreiner had made the call or if we'd look foolish showing up unannounced.

We needn't have worried. The foreman, Carlos Mondragon, was there to greet us.

"I've been expecting you," he said with a big smile.

I've been in this business more than 20 years and I continue to be amazed at how, when and where good stories, completely unexpected, will step up and kiss you right on the lips. And how utterly perfect the timing must be.

I've been in this business more than 20 years and I continue to be amazed at how, when and where good stories, completely unexpected, will step up and kiss you right on the lips.

If I hadn't noticed the little green square signifying Pioneer Park on the Spokane map, if we had given up the first time we missed the park entrance or if we had eaten lunch just a little faster, we never would have met Schreiner and his friends Adelaide and Matilda. They would be the wallaroos.

Actually, Robin and the kids first met Schreiner and the critters he calls "my babies." Robin is much better than I am at walking up and talking to perfect strangers. By the time I finished draining the cooler and joined the conversation, it had already been established who we were and what we were doing, and, more importantly, what in the world Schreiner had on his leash. He even let Robin and Melissa hold the sweet and cuddly Adelaide and Matilda, who were each 7 months old. They were so cuddly, in fact, that Jack announced he wanted to sleep with a wallaroo. I hope his stuffed kitty wasn't listening.

Schreiner gave us a crash course in baby wallaroos. How they eat (he feeds them bottles of formula every four or five hours, in addition to carrots, leaves and grass), how they sleep (in the backpack, simulating a mother's pouch, draped over the doorknob of his bedroom) and how they poop (you don't need to know).

Wallaroos are the third-largest species of kangaroos, he said. Females, such as Adelaide and Matilda, will grow to about three feet tall and weigh 50 pounds.

There are only a few breeders nationally, said Schreiner, who hopes to make some money raising wallaroos.

"I think they're going to be the next rage," he said, pulling a photo album of wallaroos from the trunk of his car to show us. "They're so nice."

Schreiner knows a little about rages and exotic animals. He made money off pot-bellied pigs and emus. He's a businessman, but he's also an animal-lover. I asked how he came to own a ranch stocked with exotic animals and he replied, essentially, because he can.

He has the interest and the money.

And we had an invitation.

The next morning, Mondragon piled us into a Jeep and carted us around the ranch of golden hills with a stupendous view, back across the Columbia, of Oregon's Mount Hood. This is part breeding farm, part petting zoo and part family hobby for the Schreiners.

Actually, Robin and the kids first met Schreiner and the critters he calls "my babies." She's much better than I at walking up and talking to perfect strangers.

And the animals have lots of room to roam.

It was relentlessly windy— typical conditions for the Columbia River Gorge — as Mondragon showed us pheasants and reindeer and buffalo. We fed deer from Japan and rainbow trout in a pond. The kids petted donkeys. A camel kissed me.

And never have I been so close to so much yak doo.

We met Larry the Elk. Up close. Actually his name is Lawrence W. Elk (get it?).

"He's the friendly one," said Carlos. "You will get a good picture."

He was and we did.

The rest of the elk have been shipped to a sister ranch in Idaho. Only Larry and one other elk remain at Dallesport.

The ranch is private and not officially open to the public, but Schreiner doesn't mind motorists driving onto the ranch for a look, their curiosity aroused by the sight of zebras on the hillsides behind the tall fences. He invites school groups for tours. He makes visits to schools and nursing homes with his wallaroos.

And, fortunately for us, he also takes his wallaroos for walks in the park.

Dallesport (http://klickitatcounty.org/Tourism/about)
The Dalles (http://www.el.com/To/TheDalles)
Schreiner Farms (http://www.idahomall.com/elkcompany)

We met Larry the Elk. Up close. Actually his name is Lawrence W. Elk (get it?).

Oregon's reception was more than chilly

NEWPORT, Ore. — Mark Twain said the coldest winter he ever spent was a summer in San Francisco.

He obviously never camped on the Oregon coast in July.

Surf's up! And where did you put my long johns?

Cold, foggy and windy are the conditions we encountered. I know we'll get misty over the memory of the chill when we're baking in Death Valley, but we were too busy shivering at the time to appreciate it.

I asked a helpful woman at an Oregon visitors' center — she had just recommended what turned out to be an excellent seafood place — whether the weather was abnormal, and she acknowledged it was.

"This," she said, "is more like August."

Oh.

Mild complaints aside, this place is beautiful. The beach is rocky in spots with cliffs hugging the shore, yet wide and sandy in others. The views here should hang in an art gallery. No swimmers, though. A few brave souls waded in up to their knees, but you could count them on one mitten. When you come to the Oregon beaches in the summer, you bring a sweater, camera and kite, not your Kermit the Frog inner tube.

We had entered Oregon from the north, swooping down through the wheat fields and sagebrush of southeast Washington. We spent a night in The Dalles, a historic trading post on the brawny Columbia River, which, with its many dams, is both a source of electricity for residents and a source of consternation among those who don't appreciate wild rivers being tamed.

Dams or not, driving along the Columbia River Gorge is one impressive ride. And forever windy. In places, the road winds close to the river as sheer cliffs rise straight up from the highway.

We drove across Bridge of the Gods that spans the Columbia, and, on the way to Portland, veered off on a side road featuring a series of waterfalls, including the spectacular, double-decker Multnomah Falls.

We made a stop in Portland to see a friendly face, Danielle White, a former Richmonder who moved to the great Northwest a few years ago and works at a grocery store featuring organically

Surf's up! And where did you put my long johns?

grown food. She also happened to catch the bouquet at our wedding almost 16 years ago.

Danielle had prepared a CARE package for us of homemade zucchini bread, fruit and other goodies. She also served as our mailbox on the road, as my mother had shipped her a few items that needed our attention.

Then it was on to the coast, winding through small town after small town before we reached Lincoln City, where the sun was melting into the Pacific.

Lewis and Clark couldn't have been any happier to see the Pacific.

In his diary, Clark scribbled, "Ocian in view! O! the joy."

Amen, brother.

I just hope he remembered to pack his Polartec jacket on the back of his horse. And that he got here before closing time at one of the ubiquitous little roadside stands where you can buy the unlikely combination of an espresso and a hot dog.

We pulled Big Blue to an oceanfront parking spot and unleashed our herd from the van. Despite the cold, they made a brief run to the water. This is not quite the halfway point of our trip, but it is probably the biggest milestone. They had been staring at the big patch of blue on the left side of their maps for months. And now they were finally here.

Melissa was slightly taken aback and a little disillusioned by the cold wind and the chilly water. According to all of the television shows featuring California beaches, the Pacific is a warm and sunny place. Or so she thought.

Their feet wet and sandy, the kids returned to the van for a ride of another few minutes to our campsite at a state park.

It was cold and dark — and we were tired — when we arrived, so we slept in the van that night. It wasn't exactly like sleeping in a four-star hotel and we can't spread out because of all of the stuff we brought, but it wasn't bad.

The next day, though, was certainly a highlight of our visit: a trip to the Oregon Coast Aquarium in Newport, the former home of Keiko the killer whale, the star of "Free Willy" and "Free Willy II" who now resides in Iceland.

The kids got up close and personal with anemones and sea urchins, and Jack and Alex decided they have a favorite jellyfish: blue jellies, which are tiny, edible creatures from the tropical Pacific that aren't exceedingly blue but are pretty cute. For jellyfish.

We pulled Big Blue to an oceanfront parking spot and unleashed our herd from the van. Despite the cold, they made a brief run to the water.

As Easterners, we enjoyed the emphasis on Pacific water life and found the exhibits entertaining and educational, with the accompanying descriptions and explanations helpfully clear.

The centerpiece of the aquarium is its new Passages of the Deep, a $6.9 million, 1.32-million gallon exhibit that opened in the spring and is in the enormous custom-made tank that previously housed Keiko.

Visitors stroll through a 200-foot clear, acrylic, underwater tunnel, which allows them to come face to face with a variety of marine life, including seldom-seen, cold-water sharks. It gives you the sensation of walking on the ocean floor.

We camped two nights on the Oregon coast and took long walks along several beaches, checking out the rocks, peering into the tide pools and avoiding the chilly surf. It was pretty and far different than what we've come to expect from the Outer Banks. Still, we could not escape the cold and dampness, which are typical for the coast, although the temperatures during our stay — highs in the 50s — were a little cool even for Oregon.

Jack rolled out of his sleeping bag one morning, shaking in his pajamas. He emerged from the tent into the morning chill and had one request for Robin before breakfast:

"Turn off the coldness."

Columbia River Gorge (http://www.fs.fed.us/r6/columbia)
Bridge of the Gods (http://www.teleport.com/%7Esisemo/legends/bridge_gods.htm)
Oregon Coast Aquarium (http://www.aquarium.org)
Oregon Tourism Commission (http://www.traveloregon.com)

Jack rolled out of his sleeping bag one morning, shaking in his pajamas. He ... had one request for Robin before breakfast: "Turn off the coldness."

Time traveling is a state of mind

ON THE ROAD — On a fast-moving, cross-country trip, your perspective changes. You begin to think less in terms of days and dates and more in terms of states.

Like the time I dug a bag of bagels of questionable origin out of the food box in the van.

"What state are they from?" asked Robin.

I thought a minute.

"Iowa."

We were in Wyoming at the time.

Bye-bye bagels.

Or the evening Jack asked if he needed to take a bath.

"No," Robin told our relieved son, "you can take a bath in Idaho."

Now that we've reached the Pacific coast, having driven almost 5,000 miles in less than four weeks, and are, in a sense, headed home, I thought I'd address a number of questions that have arisen, including this one:

What are the kids doing on those long rides?

Robin and I came up with a list of about 30 things they are doing, a third of which involve some sort of complaining: too hot, too cold, too thirsty, too hungry, can't find something, can't see anything, need to use the bathroom, etc.

They're not spending all of their time griping. Sometimes they're sniping. They call each other names, push each other a few times, and then they get all lovey-dovey. It's really rather disgusting but as long as they're quiet and there's no blood, I don't care.

Honestly, though, they've been generally pretty constructive in the way they spend their time. They're also: reading, drawing, singing silly songs; playing make-believe with their stuffed animals (Alex and Jack); listening to adolescent CDs through headphones (Melissa), looking for state license plates (we still need Hawaii); pointing out tractors (for Jack), pointing out horses (for Alex), pointing out McDonald's (for Melissa; overwhelmed, she actually stopped counting around Indiana); sleeping a little, watching television in the van even less (although they seem the most content watching tapes of "The Brady Bunch" episodes), and writing in their journals; we've listened to a

Now that we've reached the Pacific coast, having driven almost 5,000 miles in less than four weeks, and are, in a sense, headed home, I thought I'd address a number of questions that have arisen …

variety of music, a learn-Spanish-while-you-drive CD (we can ask, "Where do you catch the train for Madrid?") and a few homemade tunes from the back of the van, courtesy of a kiddie keyboard we brought along.

We seem to spend entirely too much time waiting for everyone to buckle their seat-belts and get happy before shoving off in the van. I estimate we've spent the equivalent of two days — engine idling, teeth gritting — sitting in parking places, listening to someone in the back say, "I can't get buckled!" or "I won't get buckled!" or "I don't want to sit in this seat!"

Sometimes, their complaints come in the form of a request and are actually well-meaning.

The other day while we were riding, Jack asked for an apple. Robin found the paring knife and began peeling it for him. Jack reminded her to wash the knife — we were going 70 mph at the time — because he didn't want to "get any germs."

Jack, my man, the floor of the van is littered with water bottles we've all shared, we've slept a number of nights in a small tent like socks in a drawer, we've gone stretches of days without hot baths, and we've used public bathrooms in every state we've visited (including Montana where soap isn't an option in the official state rest stops we enjoyed). I think we're well past worrying about germs. I'm just hoping all of our vaccinations kick in.

We've shipped home three boxes of belongings — the third was sent during a UPS stop in Portland — to create more room in the van, but we've also added a few necessities. We stopped at a WalMart in Bozeman, Mont., to buy jeans for Melissa and socks for Jack and Alex. We bought a plastic washtub at a camp store for cleaning our campsite dishes. We've purchased four million postcards, most of which will never be mailed.

We've also lost a few things along the way, including Robin's wide-angle camera lens. We think it's somewhere in Iowa. Or Nebraska. Or maybe, we're hoping, in one of the boxes we shipped home.

Alex lost a tooth in Yellowstone and almost an eye in Oregon. Her buddy Jack tossed a rock that caught her on the side of the face. That was a harbinger of things to come that day. Despite the long days and the long drives, we have done fairly well at keeping our sense of humor. But that day, somewhere along the Pacific Coast Highway in Oregon, between Newport and Coos Bay, we lost it. All of us. We were fussing and fuming with each other in an awful way. I was ready to walk into a UPS office and have myself shipped home.

I think we're well past worrying about germs. I'm just hoping all of our vaccinations kick in.

But a good night's sleep helped everyone.

Sleep is something we're all about a quart low on. There is so much we want to do and see — and so many miles we have to travel to stick to our itinerary — we often show up at motels and campgrounds late and then try to get going fairly early the next morning.

Camping also has taken its toll. On the last day of a long stretch of scheduled camping, we drove into Humboldt Redwoods State Park in northern California, an awesomely beautiful place where the campsites are tucked into a grove of second-growth redwoods (sunburn is not an issue). We set up our tent, at which point Alex declared, in fairly teary tones, she would "not sleep again inside anything that was zipped." She curled up in the back seat of the van and slept peacefully.

Somewhere amid all of this driving and sightseeing and exploring, I have to write stories and shoot photographs and transmit both back to the paper. It's only a matter of time when we're staying in motels; I'm often up until 1 or 2 in the morning writing and filing after a full day of travel.

But in campgrounds the long hours get even more complicated, and I start getting real sentimental about electrical outlets and phone jacks. I've spent a number of cold nights sitting at campground picnic tables, well after midnight, the campfire still crackling, typing stories and editing pictures — until my batteries run low. I've recharged my laptop and camera batteries in campground bathrooms, with the kids serving as lookouts to make sure nobody makes off with them.

Among the places I've begged phone lines to transmit are the concierge desk at a lodge in Yellowstone National Park where we weren't staying, a ranger station at a campground in California where we were, and the Oregon Coast Aquarium, where the folks on duty not only found a phone jack for me in an out-of-the-way place, but also set up a make-shift desk with a chair and a stool.

Strangely, a month into this trip — an exceedingly long time away from home for us — we are not terribly homesick. I felt sure we would be, the kids especially. We miss our family and friends — and we miss our beds — but we are not desperately longing for home. Maybe it's because we're moving so fast and every day we're going somewhere new and doing something different.

Still, there are times when Jack will say, "Mommy, I'm thinking about my room and my toys."

He's apparently thinking about other things too.

The other day, we were rolling through the farmland of southeastern Washington state, admiring the amber waves of grain, when Jack asked about one of the things he misses most.

We set up our tent, at which point Alex declared, in fairly teary tones, she would "not sleep again inside anything that was zipped."

A truck? A book? His sandbox?

Nope. The litle gizmo we have that slices cheddar and Monterey jack.

"Mommy," he said, "did you bring the cheese-cutter?"

Afraid not.

Humboldt Redwoods State Park (http://parks.ca.gov/north/ncrd/hrsp.html)

"Mommy," he said, "did you bring the cheese-cutter?"

We saw ups and downs of San Francisco

SAN FRANCISCO — We sailed beneath the Golden Gate Bridge, we hung on for dear life aboard a cable car and we ate one of our best meals ever.

And what our children probably will remember most about our visit to San Francisco was playing with pigeons.

Pigeons.

We've driven 5,000 miles and come to one of the world's great cities — to chase and pet and be thoroughly entertained by birds that I once heard described as "rats with wings."

I've been a parent long enough to not be surprised by this. Amazed but not surprised.

We frolicked with the pigeons outside the Exploratorium, a gigantic science museum, with more than 650 interactive exhibits, all housed at the historic and stately Palace of Fine Arts.

We'd spent a lovely morning at the Exploratorium, where the kids bounced from one exhibit to another and didn't want to leave. We ate a picnic lunch in the shadow of nearby Golden Gate Bridge and were walking back past the museum to snap a few photographs before catching the bus to Fisherman's Wharf where we were staying.

That's when we saw the pigeons. Dozens of them. Maybe millions. I lost count. One little girl was picking up the birds and holding them. Cuddling them like dolls. Two, then three, finally four at a time.

I was contemplating this scene, trying to determine if it was the West Coast people or the birds that were different than their East Coast counterparts. Next thing I knew, Jack and Alex were chasing the pigeons, trying to catch them. I was rooting for the birds.

Then a nice older woman showed up with a bag of seed she happily shared with all of the kids, including ours. (Except for Melissa, who ran for cover beneath a nearby shade tree and watched in horror as her siblings raced closer and closer to the birds.)

But feeding these creatures wasn't merely enough. Robin scooped up a pigeon for Alex to pet. I thought I'd seen everything. Then — and this was truly the cherry on the sundae — a pigeon landed on the Times-Dispatch cap I was wearing. I've yet to determine if this was a metaphor for something very deep. I hope not.

At least the bird didn't disgrace himself on my hat.

I've been a parent long enough to not be surprised by this. Amazed but not surprised.

San Francisco was a memorable stop for more reasons than just overly friendly birds.

We took a chilly, hour-long cruise into San Francisco Bay that carried us beneath the Golden Gate Bridge and around the island of Alcatraz that was once a notorious prison but is now the most popular tourist attraction in the city. There is a waiting list to get into the place now, which is just the opposite of the way it used to be.

The bay is a brisk place, to put it charitably. We huddled on the top deck of the boat, which hopped through choppy seas on its way to the bridge. The ride was a lot smoother, and even a little warmer — and less of an adventure —on the return with the wicked wind at our backs.

Brisk is also a good way to describe San Francisco in general during the summer. A friend who lives in California and visits San Francisco from time to time said he always winds up buying his wife a jacket when they come to the city because she underestimates the cold. The first night, we thought it funny the souvenir shops along Fisherman's Wharf sold not only T-shirts but fleece jackets. Didn't seem so funny when we bought fleece jackets the next day — to wear on top of the fleece jackets we'd brought with us.

We strolled through Chinatown and into, I believe, every shop on Grant Avenue, looking to see which one was selling postcards 12 for a dollar or had the best deal on T-shirts or other trinkets. I view this form of shopping in the same way I look at going from one yard sale to another, which I consider only a step removed from a root canal. The rest of the members of my family, however, consider this almost as enthralling as handling pigeons.

I enjoyed Chinatown, but I was more interested in the food. We found a little walk-up restaurant, where we ate soup and fried rice. It must have been good because Alex and Jack, who are not big fans of Chinese food, enjoyed it, too. They even used chopsticks.

Dinner in Chinatown was only a warm-up for the next night, however, when we visited Alioto's, one of San Francisco's best-known restaurants. The venerable, family-run seafood house on Fisherman's Wharf is known for its food, service and view of the bay — a dining trifecta.

What I enjoyed most, though, was a conversation with our waiter. Alex and Jack are picky eaters, so it was a bit of a risk going to a nice place with linen tablecloths and waiters in tuxes but no deep-fried chicken parts that come with fries and a toy.

The menu included elaborate dishes involving tortellini and penne pasta. The kids love the pasta but not the sauces. I asked if it would be possible to just order plates of plain pasta.

I view this form of shopping in the same way I look at going from one yard sale to another, which I consider only a step removed from a root canal.

"Anything is possible," the waiter told me.

Big tip time.

 (I elected not to pass along Jack's request for "parmesan in the green can." The waiter brought parmesan in a silver dish, which went over just as well.)

We all cleaned our plates, and nobody burped. A great meal.

We spent three nights in San Francisco, staying at the Marriott Fisherman's Wharf, which gave us easy access to places along the wharf such as Ghirardelli Square — a former chocolate factory that's been transformed into shops and restaurants — and Pier 39, which is also a shopping and eating place and even has a carousel and something no place else in town can boast: dozens of resident sea lions cavorting on floating docks. A few years back when the sea lions first showed up, some merchants considered them pests; now they're tourist magnets.

San Francisco is one of those places you could spend weeks in and still not do everything. We missed several museums we had hoped to visit, as well as the new Pac Bell Park, home of the San Francisco Giants baseball team. We'd hoped to visit Pac Bell on our way out of town. We got within a couple of blocks of the park when I took a wrong turn and we found ourselves on the San Francisco Oakland Bay Bridge traveling 55 mph. A U-turn would have been difficult.

Despite what we missed, we did a lot. Including driving the hilly streets of San Francisco. I crested one hill and was transported, just for a moment, to Paramount's Kings Dominion's Rebel Yell. Thought for sure I was in the front seat — although I resisted the urge to raise my arms and scream. We also navigated Big Blue down Lombard Street, the "world's crookedest street." Twice.

And while walking to our hotel from Chinatown one evening, we stumbled upon the North Beach Playground, where the children had a big time for a few minutes. It was just a playground, but our kids are just kids. Same goes for pigeons.

Exploratorium (http://www.exploratorium.edu)
Palace of Fine Arts (http://www.exploratorium.edu/palace/index.html)
Alcatraz (http://www.nps.gov/alcatraz/welcome.html)
Alioto's (http://www.fishermanswharf.org/Alioto.htm)
Fisherman's Wharf (http://www.fishermanswharf.org/)
Ghiradelli Square (http://www.ghirardellisq.com)
Pier 39 (http://www.pier39.com)

A few years back when the sea lions first showed up, some merchants considered them pests; now they're tourist magnets.

Yosemite's stars (and visitors) are countless

YOSEMITE NATIONAL PARK, Calif. — In a wilderness that in the daylight seems very nearly overrun with humans, we found a place after dark that felt as if we had it all to ourselves.

Sitting on a blanket in a meadow in Yosemite Valley, we gazed up into the ceiling of stars, peering into the Milky Way and playing connect-the-dots with constellations.

We were along with a small group for a Starry Skies Over Yosemite program, led by Leland Hales, a geologist, paleontologist and zoologist by training and an astronomer by passion. He transported us to another world without leaving the valley.

It was a peaceful end to a hectic day — and just about the most fun we had during our stay at Yosemite National Park, one of the true gems in the park system.

Because of its awe-inspiring beauty and wonderful hiking trails, Yosemite is one busy place. Four million visitors come each year, the majority of them to Yosemite Valley, which is seven miles long, one mile wide and surrounded by sheer granite walls. A river, the Merced, runs through it. And the valley features a number of breathtaking waterfalls, including Yosemite Falls, the tallest in North America at 2,425 feet.

It's easy to see why so many people flock to this place. It's also easy to see why, at peak times, it can be so hard to get around.

In fact, the National Park Service is in the process of planning Yosemite's future. It's under a directive to reduce traffic congestion and crowding, while at the same time trying to make the park as accessible as possible to as many as possible.

This is what's known as a thorny issue.

Thank goodness all we had to do was just enjoy the park — and try to get from one place to another, which wasn't too terribly easy at times. Free shuttle buses transport visitors around the valley in an effort to reduce congestion. It's a fine idea and the buses run frequently, but there were just so many people when we were there that the buses were crammed at times. It had the feel of the New York subway.

"If you weren't close friends when you got on," a cheery bus driver told a standing-room-only, flesh-to-flesh crowd, including us, "you will be by the time you get off."

I was standing in the back of the bus, squeezed between a number of people, one hand hanging

It's easy to see why so many people flock to this place. It's also easy to see why, at peak times, it can be so hard to get around.

on to a handrail, the other clutching a camera. That's when it felt like a bug began crawling up my pants leg. But I couldn't move and I had no free hands. Only way I could find out for sure if it was an insect was to ask the guy behind me to check. Despite what the driver said, I didn't feel we were *that* close. I decided to live with the bug.

At least it wasn't a bear. Bears have become a serious problem in Yosemite. Actually, it's people who are the problem. Bears have grown accustomed to human food and, with so many visitors in the valley, they know where to find it.

We've heard bear warnings in Yellowstone and Glacier national parks, but neither had the restrictions of Yosemite, where visitors are required to remove all food from their cars — groceries, coolers, stray French fries beneath the car seat. Bears have good sniffers and powerful muscles. In 1999, bears broke into more than 300 cars in the park.

We cleaned out the van. We saw no bears.

We'd come to Yosemite from San Francisco. At the end of the last century, that was a five-day ride by stagecoach. These days, it's little more than four hours. Unless you were riding with us as we tried to replicate the days of stage-coach travel. Our trip took a good seven hours, including several restroom breaks, two incidents of motion sickness and a wrong turn. But the scenery was nice.

In the park, we stayed at Yosemite Lodge, a motel-like accommodation in the valley that was most comfortable and convenient. We took a two-hour valley tour aboard an open-air tram with a would-be comedian as a guide. He was quite entertaining. In between his funny lines and stories, he also was pretty informative.

While the park is forever linked to names such as John Muir, Ansel Adams and Theodore Roosevelt, our guide told us it was actually Abraham Lincoln who saved the place. In 1864, Lincoln set aside what is now Yosemite as a grant to the state of California, just as a group of pioneers was scheming to blow up the valley's granite walls to do who-knows-what. This was the first federal authorization to preserve scenic lands for public benefit and was the basis for the later concept of state and national park systems.

We visited the Happy Isles Nature Center, where Jack held a huge sugar pine cone, the likes of which can grow to two feet in length and weigh five pounds. We hiked a few short trails, visited a couple of waterfalls. It is amazing how quickly Jack's legs get tired and he needs a piggyback ride —

It is amazing how quickly Jack's legs get tired and he needs a piggy-back ride — and how contagious his weariness is to Alex, who also is quick to request a lift.

and how contagious his weariness is to Alex, who also is quick to request a lift.

One of the best things we've done at several of the national parks, including Yosemite, is encourage Melissa and Alex to participate in the junior ranger programs. It's provided good incentive for them to stay interested during our visits. Jack, too. In Yosemite, he received a button for helping the girls collect a bag of trash.

The junior ranger programs typically require researching questions specific to the park, becoming familiar with who and what lives there, going along on a ranger-led event, and performing a little hands-on work. The girls are mildly quizzed before being given badges by rangers, who very kindly make a bit of a big deal out of it, congratulating them and shaking their hands and even announcing their accomplishment to others in the visitors' centers.

Speaking of visitors' centers, on our last day in Yosemite we drove toward the east entrance and into the less-congested high country of the park. We stopped at Tuolumne Meadows, which, at 8,000 feet, is under a blanket of snow eight months out of the year, but in the summer is covered only with wildflowers.

At the visitors' center there, I was in line waiting to buy a book. I was wearing a Times-Dispatch shirt and a woman touched my arm and asked if I was Bill Lohmann. I must have given her the same look FBI agents get when they apprehend a fugitive on the Most Wanted List. I'm not used to being recognized beyond the Richmond suburbs, much less in the mountains of California.

Turns out it was Becky Roish of western Henrico County, who was on a California vacation with her husband Walt and daughter Melissa. She'd read the earlier stories from our trip and actually wondered if they'd run into us.

Small world, indeed.

Yosemite National Park (http://www.nps.gov/yose/home.htm)
Yosemite Lodge (http://www.nps.gov/yose/planning/gmp/lodge.html)
Happy Isles Nature Center (http://geology.csun.edu/yosemite/hi.html)
Tuolumne Meadows (http://www.sierragatewaymap.com/tmr.html)
Yosemite Concession Services Corp (http://www.yosemitepark.com)

... a woman touched my arm and asked if I was Bill Lohmann. I must have given her the same look FBI agents get when they apprehend a fugitive on the Most Wanted List.

We warmed up in Death Valley

DEATH VALLEY, Calif. — As we drove into the hottest place in the Western Hemisphere, I thought it would be cool to roll down the van's window and see just how hot it felt.

It felt like I'd opened the oven to check on the chicken.

Just about done, I'd say.

Later, when we finally got out and around, it wasn't bad at all, only about 105 degrees.

Of course, it was 10 o'clock at night.

I believe they call this the cool of the evening in Death Valley.

What a place. Death Valley is at once desolate and intimidating and utterly magnificent. And very hot. So hot, in fact, the air coming out of the automatic hand-dryers in the restaurant restroom felt like air conditioning.

We knew that going in. You don't make a reservation at Death Valley in the middle of summer and expect temperatures in the 80s. Not even for the lows. (We also didn't expect rain; less than two inches falls annually.)

But we wanted to see Death Valley and really feel the heat. It was on the way, between our last stop, Yosemite National Park, and our next one, Las Vegas. So, why not?

As we drove into Death Valley, the first thing that struck me was the roadside sign that advised motorists to turn off their air-conditioning because of the steep, uphill grade crossing the mountains into the valley. Then we started seeing big water tanks at turnouts on the side of the road for motorists with overheating radiators.

As Big Blue labored over the mountains — but never overheated — and we began perspiring, the second thing that struck me was how in the world anyone got out alive in that first party of pioneers who blundered into the valley in 1849.

They were looking for a shortcut. They found hell instead. They were trapped on a desert floor more than 200 feet below sea level, surrounded by mountains reaching as high as 11,000 feet. And they didn't have an air-conditioned conversion van.

After five weeks of thirst and near starvation, the pioneers made it out of Death Valley. Only one man died, but all of the others had their tickets punched before staggering out of the place. On departing, a woman supposedly uttered the words, "Goodbye, Death Valley."

... the second thing that struck me was how in the world anyone got out alive in that first party of pioneers who blundered into the valley in 1849.

Despite its reputation, the valley attracted those hoping to make a quick buck mining gold and silver. Neither proved to be plentiful, but there was lots of "white gold" — borax. Nowadays, the gold comes in the form of tourism.

Death Valley is the largest national park in the Lower 48. For years, it was a winter haven — the winters are actually pretty pleasant, with high temperatures in the 80s — but now air conditioning has made summer bearable as well. Mostly, anyway.

We stayed at the Furnace Creek Inn & Ranch Resort, which is an oasis in the middle of the desert. It has been open in the summer for the past few years and is routinely packed during the worst weather Death Valley can offer. The resort's golf course — billed as the world's lowest grass course — is open even during the summer; good mid-afternoon tee times are available.

The vast majority of summer visitors are European, who stop here for a night or two on their way from Las Vegas or Yosemite or Los Angeles.

"The Europeans really love our national parks," said Toni Doyle Jepson, manager of Furnace Creek. "They don't have any deserts, and they want to see our deserts at their harshest."

And there's something about being able to go home and dazzle the friends and neighbors with tales of surviving Death Valley.

"Oh, definitely!" said Jepson.

We have the T-shirts to prove it.

Jepson and her husand Cal, general manager of the resort, have lived here four years. They came from the cooler climate — well, most any place outside of a health club sauna would be cool compared to Death Valley — of Carmel. Once they got used to not having easy access to certain amenities such as dry cleaning — nearest dry-cleaning shop is about 60 miles away — they grew comfortable with the desert.

"I love it," said Toni Jepson. "It's very quiet. Kind of mystical, spiritual. It's a very different life."

Locals have a trick for dealing with the heat, she said.

"We don't look at the temperature that day to see how hot it is," she said. "We wait until the next day to find out. It's easier to take if you don't know exactly how hot it is."

It was 121° the day before, she said.

But it's a dry heat. (Yeah, right.)

It was 121°
the day before,
she said. But it's
a dry heat.
(Yeah, right.)

We swam in the pool the evening we arrived — we stayed at the comfortable but less expensive motel-like ranch; the inn has a AAA four-diamond rating and is very nice, but beyond our budget. The pool is fed by warm springs and is a constant 84 degrees, which is extremely warm by our pool standards but almost refreshing in heat beyond 120.

Next morning, Jack and Alex headed straight for the playground. Seven minutes later, they headed straight back to the room. Too hot. Unless you've been in this heat, it's a little difficult to adequately describe, although "searing" comes close.

A park ranger in Yosemite had warned us our eyes would burn the first time we stepped out in the desert. They did.

Everyone also told us to take plenty of water. We filled two five-gallon jugs plus numerous bottles.

And lots of people told us Death Valley was beautiful. They were right about that, too.

The dunes and the desert floor are intriguing, and the rock formations are absolutely stunning in the rainbow of colors revealed in their various layers: pinks, purples, emeralds and browns. We drove down a side road called Artist's Drive that took us past a large selection of these colorful formations.

"The first time I saw them," said Toni Jepson, "I fully understood Indian art and where they got their colors and designs."

We drove to Badwater, the lowest point in the Western Hemisphere at 282 feet below sea level — and sinking. Looking up at the little "sea level" sign on a nearby canyon wall gives you the desperate sensation of standing on the bottom of a pool.

There are actually small pools of water at Badwater — water containing four to five times the salt content of an ocean. We got out for the requisite photo, but not for long. This was one place the kids didn't have to be coaxed back into the van. The heat grows more intense the lower you go, and the white salt flats reflect the heat of the sun in your face. They say you can hear the dry salt floor creaking on hot days as it expands in the heat, but we didn't hang around that long.

The skies at Death Valley are typically crystal clear. The days we were there, though, the skies were somewhat hazy from wildfires elsewhere in the region. On a clear day, you can drive to Dante's View and see both the lowest point in the United States — Badwater — and the highest in the Lower 48 — Mount Whitney. But this wasn't a clear day.

Unless you've been in this heat, it's a little difficult to adequately describe, although "searing" comes close.

There is scattered vegetation and considerable wildlife, although we didn't personally see any coyotes, roadrunners, rattlesnakes and scorpions. But then, you can drive for miles and miles and not see a soul or a thing. A vast, striking nothingness.

We paid $2.32 per gallon for gas in Death Valley — the highest of the trip — but it was worth every penny. Only thing possibly more valuable was the seven-pound bag of ice. A steal at $2 per bag. You just have to make sure you hustle it into your room or cooler. If you dawdle for more than, say, 30 seconds, you just bought a lovely bag of cool water.

But the best thing in Death Valley was free. After exploring for a few hours, we stumbled, bedraggled and crazy from the heat, into the 49er Cafe at Furnace Creek for lunch. And there, on every table, was a sweating pitcher of ice water.

While we were guzzling, a couple came in and sat at the counter. They'd obviously been traveling by motorcycle across the desert. They also obviously hadn't been quite prepared for what they encountered. The woman spoke with a German accent when she asked the waitress, "When does it cool off?"

I got the feeling she was looking for an answer along the lines of "7 or 8 o'clock."

"December," said the waitress.

The woman covered her face with her hands.

I took another gulp of ice water.

Death Valley National Park (http://www.nps.gov/deva)
Furnace Creek Inn & Ranch Resort (http://www.furnacecreekresort.com/frame-pn.htm)
Badwater (http://www.coolspots.com/spots/iny/page203001.html)
Dante's View (http://geology.wr.usgs.gov/docs/usgsnps/deva/ftdan1.html)
Mount Whitney (http://www.nps.gov/seki/whitney.htm)

... she asked the waitress, "When does it cool off?"

I got the feeling she was looking for an answer along the lines of "7 or 8 o'clock."

"December," said the waitress.

Visiting Las Vegas was a gamble

LAS VEGAS, Nev. — As we strolled amid the hubbub through the endless casino at the immense MGM Grand Hotel and Casino, Alex spied something shiny on the thick carpet. She reached down and came up clutching a nickel, which she quickly pocketed.

"This is a great place to find money!" she said with excitement and expectation.

Or, as others many times her age have discovered, to lose it.

We did pretty well during our stay. We left Las Vegas a grand total of — counting Alex's nickel — 20 cents poorer.

I lost my allotted $10 gambling funds the first night and won it back the second, having started my big winning streak with a hunch and a spare quarter in my pocket.

The Lohmanns are certainly the last of the big-time gamblers.

Fortunately for us, you don't have to bet the grocery money to enjoy yourself in Vegas .

Gambling, of course, built Las Vegas and it's still the primary reason most people flock to this shimmering island in the desert. But the city has evolved in recent years into sort of an amusement park with a serious edge.

That would explain why so many of the hotels have roller coasters. Yes, roller coasters.

During our visit, we saw lots of families with young children walking around town. I also saw a few of the hard-core, grizzled, whisky-drinking gamblers hunched over slot machines or sitting at blackjack tables, with the long ash of an ignored cigarette dangling from their lips.

But that was when I was strolling through the casino of the MGM Grand, where we stayed, at 3 o'clock one morning. Don't ask why. I'm still not sure. But I can tell you this: it's very tempting having a casino downstairs from your room — even with a severely limited budget of gambling money.

At any rate, the slot machines were still humming and the cards were still being dealt, although the crowd had thinned considerably from earlier in the evening. Even the strip — Las Vegas Boulevard — was fairly deserted. Las Vegas might be a town that never sleeps, but it apparently rests.

However, a thin crowd is still a crowd at the MGM Grand, where there are more than 5,000

We left Las Vegas a grand total of ... 20 cents poorer ... The Lohmanns are certainly the last of the big-time gamblers.

guest rooms and the casino is the size of four football fields. Which is just about what you'd expect from a hotel that bills itself as "the city of entertainment."

Under the MGM Grand roof is a shopping mall, a habitat inhabited by actual lions, numerous restaurants (from Emeril Lagasse's New Orleans Fish House to McDonald's), and several theaters for big-time acts, plus an arena that seats more than 17,000. There is also a six-acre water complex, which includes five pools, waterfalls and a 1,000-foot "river" where you can float away the day and either rest up for the coming evening in casino land or recuperate from the damage you did the night before.

You literally don't need to leave the place, which I imagine was the thinking behind creating such a mammoth resort in a town where the competition among hotels is fierce.

The pool complex got our attention and was where we spent most of a day. We've stayed in a number of motels with pools on this trip, but we haven't had much time for swimming. This was our splash splurge. And it was excellent timing, coming on the heels of a couple of days in Death Valley. A pool of cold water never looked so good.

We ventured out one evening onto the "strip," wandering up and down the street, stopping to buy postcards, pausing to marvel at the dancing waters at the Bellagio resort. We roamed into a couple of hotels and even rode a monorail from Bally's back to the MGM Grand.

I'd never visited Vegas, but years back I can't imagine the "strip" would have made my Top 10 list of destinations where I might want to haul my kids. It's still not quite Sunday school, but it seems fairly tame and it's certainly an eyeful. The neon, the people, the money. It's a mesmerizing place.

There was no fear and loathing, although some members of our party had their moments.

Before leaving Las Vegas, we had two important errands to run.

The first was to a local UPS pickup center where we unloaded all of our cold-weather clothes — they were required in San Francisco, Oregon and the northern Rockies but would be no longer needed as we headed south — and many of our dirty ones, shipping home three boxes of stuff. We celebrated our newfound space in Big Blue by, naturally, buying more stuff.

Which brings me to our second errand.

All along the West Coast, we'd seen people riding cute little foot-propelled scooters that fold up into a neat package. I'm sure they're all over the East Coast, as well, but we're not particularly hip

The neon, the people, the money. It's a mesmerizing place.

or observant so we'd never seen them. Anyway, the kids took a liking to them and we weren't sure we'd be able to find them back home so we purchased three as advance birthday presents.

So, we spent our last hour in Las Vegas — a city of risk and glamour and glitz — hunting for a Toys R Us.

I think that's more pathetic than losing 20 cents on the slots.

MGM Grand Hotel (http://www.mgmgrand.com/lv/pages/index_home.shtml)
Bellagio Resort (http://las.vegas.hotelguide.net/data/h100011.htm)
Bally's (http://www.ballyslv.com/)
Las Vegas Convention & Visitors Authority (http://www.lasvegas24hours.com)

I think that's more pathetic than losing 20 cents on the slots.

Grand Canyon is breathtaking

GRAND CANYON, Ariz. — Even if you've never been there, you know what's waiting for you at the Grand Canyon. Its reputation precedes it.

However, once you get there and see for yourself, the place still takes your breath away.

Walk up to the rim, peer out over the miles and miles of sheer rock faces and deep crevices, gaze up at the cottony banks of clouds and then down, way down, for a glimpse of the Colorado River, a twisting blue ribbon far below.

And, under your breath, just say, "Wow."

Calling the Grand Canyon a big hole in the ground is not necessarily inaccurate, just very, very inadequate.

We drove into Grand Canyon National Park at night. Robin was at the wheel as we sped down a two-lane road toward the south rim. Although dark thoughts crossed our mind, we just assumed there would be signs to steer us away from the edge. Our assumptions were right but it was still kind of worrisome.

The South Rim is the more crowded of the Grand Canyon vantage points. For us, though, it was also the most conveniently located because of our itinerary. We were coming from Las Vegas, by way of Hoover Dam, which was an impressive sight but largely a disappointment.

With only a couple of hours to spend, we found there was little for us to do at Hoover Dam. Tours are offered for a fee, but the wait was too long. And there was even a line — and a pretty steep admission charge — just to get into the visitors' center, after already paying to park.

We opted for a free stroll along the bridge going over the dam, snapped a few photographs, climbed back into Big Blue and continued on our way.

We ran into very little rain on our trip. Most of it came in Arizona, which I wouldn't have figured. En route to the Grand Canyon, we drove in and out of showers and were entertained by lightning as it danced across the desert.

It was dark and late when we arrived at the Grand Canyon, long after the time I'd feel safe having Jack and Alex roam around the rim. We unpacked our things at Maswik Lodge, which is among the less expensive national park accommodations, about a half-mile from the rim.

First order of business: break out the new scooters we'd purchased earlier in the day in Las

... under your breath, just say, "Wow."

Vegas. So, before bed, the kids rode around the motel room on their scooters. They wanted to ride them the next day as we went sightseeing along the rim.

I don't think so.

Next morning, Robin rose before the rest of us and walked over for our first view of the Grand Canyon. She arrived just in time to see a caravan of mules depart with their riders down a trail toward the canyon floor.

Mule rides are famous at the Grand Canyon. Half-day, daylong and overnight trail trips are offered, but reservations are required long in advance — sometimes as much as a year.

To me, there's something a little unsettling about riding any beast down the steep, narrow canyon trails, but, after hearing and reading about these creatures, if you've got to entrust your safety to a beast, it might as well be a mule.

Mules are the result of unions between male donkeys and female horses. They bite, but they don't slip. Their sure-footedness — and cooperative nature — led one knowledgeable man to proclaim the difference between riding a horse and a mule as comparable to the difference between riding a washing machine and a Cadillac.

We didn't have time for a mule trip, which didn't really matter because small kids aren't allowed to ride anyway. But we enjoyed seeing a group of mules and their riders return later in the afternoon, slowly but surely ascending Bright Angel trail. I overheard one woman, after dismounting, describe her mule trip as "The best thing I've ever done."

A mule ride would have been fun, and sometime I'd love to go back and ride down into the canyon. Hiking Bright Angel or one of the other trails would have been equally enjoyable. But the trails descend fairly quickly and we worried about Alex and Jack, in particular, safely negotiating them. The Grand Canyon didn't strike us as a place to take unnecessary chances.

So, we walked along the edge of the South Rim — Jack's hand firmly in one of ours — and took in the views. Everyone's seen photographs of the place, but standing there and staring out over the vastness is an entirely different experience.

The South Rim is fairly crowded, with lodges built almost to the edge, but the tourists are not really elbow-to-elbow. Relative solitude is close by, if you're willing to hike a short distance down any of the trails. Next time, I will.

Once again, that pesky Arizona weather caught us on our way out of the park. A late afternoon

… I overheard one woman describe her mule trip as "The best thing I've ever done."

thunderstorm swept in, kicking up winds, throwing bucketfuls of rain, and casting shadows across the canyon. The changing colors of the sky and red rock kept pulling us off the road and into every scenic viewpoint as we drove along the East Rim.

As we neared the end of the East Rim road and were about to make a turn away from the Grand Canyon and toward our next stop in central Arizona, Alex beseeched us to make one more stop and climb out of the van one more time in order to take one last look.

"I want to say goodbye to the Grand Canyon," she said.

Standing in the wind and the rain, we all did exactly that.

Grand Canyon National Park (http://www.nps.gov/grca)
Hoover Dam (http://www.hooverdam.com)
Maswik Lodge (http://www.grand-canyon.az.us/serv/gc_pl_ml.htm)

Alex beseeched us to make one more stop and climb out of the van one more time in order to take one last look.

"I want to say goodbye to the Grand Canyon," she said.

Hanging out in Winslow, AZ

WINSLOW, Ariz. — This is the town that turned standing on a corner into art.

And just maybe into its salvation.

The corner of Second Street and Kinsley Avenue — along what used to be known as "the mother road," Route 66 — has been designated as *The Corner*.

Well, I'm a-standin' on a corner

in Winslow, Arizona,

Such a fine sight to see;

It's a girl, my Lord,

In a flatbed Ford

Slowin' down

To take a look at me.

Glenn Frey and Jackson Browne wrote "Take It Easy," and the Eagles turned it into their first big hit, putting themselves and Winslow on the map.

Now, almost 30 years later, the good folks of Winslow — a town down for years, but not out — is finally trying to capitalize on it.

Winslow, 60 miles east of Flagstaff, has established a park — Standin' on The Corner Park — that features an optical illusion of a mural on a bare brick wall that depicts the song lyrics, as well as a life-size bronze statue of a young man, standing on the corner, with his guitar.

We had "Take It Easy" blaring on the van's stereo system when we rolled into Winslow late at night, Jack and Alex leading the chorus from the back, although Jack still insists the girl is driving a "fat bed Ford."

The next morning, the five of us stood on *The Corner*. I'm not sure it was the spiritual experience for the rest of my family that it was for me, but I had the van keys in my pocket.

The park is small as parks go, but it means a lot to Winslow, particularly the historic downtown area that had fallen into disrepair as time and travelers passed it by. In fact, the park was a vacant lot before its rebirth.

"It's given us a pride that you can't explain," said Yvonne Howeth, a member of the committee

I'm not sure it was the spiritual experience for the rest of my family that it was for me, but I had the van keys in my pocket.

that planned, built and maintains the park, which opened last September. "The town loves it.

"People have started cleaning up their buildings, people have started buying buildings," said Howeth, as she, her husband Glenn and I stood in the morning sun at the park. "The park has done nothing but good."

Tom McCauley, also a member of the park committee, can recall the precise moment Winslow lost its pulse.

Oct. 28, 1978, 4 p.m.

"I can still remember that as the day the town died," said McCauley.

That's when Interstate 40 — nearby, but not near enough — opened, diverting traffic, business and the future around the town.

Winslow used to be a vital stop along old Route 66, the popular path taken by so many seeking fame, fortune and a new life on the West Coast. The town was a major depot for the Santa Fe Railway. And Charles Lindbergh designed the airport, which is big enough to accommodate a 737.

Winslow was a thriving town. But people stopped riding trains, and planes began flying farther, bypassing Winslow. The interstate drove a nail in Winslow's coffin.

"The interstates have killed small towns like that," Eagles drummer Don Henley told my colleague, Times-Dispatch music writer Melissa Ruggieri a few months ago.

When approached by Howeth's committee, Henley, who grew up in a small town in Texas, provided the seed money to build the park.

"God bless them if it helps them revive something," said Henley.

The revival began in 1997 when La Posada, the town's grand hotel and one of the grandest anywhere, reopened after being closed for 40 years.

La Posada, two blocks from *The Corner* and just on the other side of downtown Winslow's only traffic light, was opened in 1930 as a great railroad hotel. The Santa Fe Railway depot was just beyond its terrace. The hotel was the property of the Fred Harvey Co., an outfit that civilized travel in the West.

La Posada, large and rambling, was designed as if it were a hacienda belonging to a fabulously wealthy Spanish Don. The huge hotel cost $2 million to construct, a staggering sum for its time.

This was a retreat for the rich and famous — Howard Hughes, John Wayne, Bob Hope, Albert

Oct. 28, 1978, 4 p.m. "I can still remember that as the day the town died," said McCauley.

Einstein. Later, stars such as Frank Sinatra, Dorothy Lamour and Jackie Gleason entertained soldiers here when Winslow was a major transport stop during World War II. Some days, thousands of short-haired, fuzzy-cheeked young men stopped in Winslow long enough to venture into La Posada for a Coke and a Spam sandwich before going off to war in the Pacific theater.

Winslow — and Spam — may have been their last taste of home.

La Posada flamed out quickly, closing in 1957. It was nearly demolished several times, with townspeople fighting to save it. At one point, a group of volunteers — known as the Gardening Angels — would show up regularly to weed and mow the once exquisite grounds, just to keep it respectable.

Finally, in 1997, a deal was struck among representatives of the railroad, the state, the town and Allan Affeldt, a fellow who once led peace marches in Russia and who, as his partner Daniel Lutzick said, "makes things happen." Besides Lutzick, a sculptor, Affeldt's other partner is his wife Tina Mion, a painter.

The place, still undergoing renovation, has an artsy feel, but also a homey one.

We stayed at La Posada — the rates are remarkably reasonable — in the Frank Sinatra Suite. You can help yourself to ice from the freezer and books from the library. The kids made themselves at home in the basement game room. It was like staying at the home of a filthy rich uncle, who leaves chocolates on your pillow, although I don't happen to have an uncle like that.

After La Posada reopened its doors, the town's focus turned toward the park, which, based on what they can tell from Frey's memory of coming through Winslow years ago, is on *the* corner.

The central piece of the park is the mural. The artist, John Pugh of Los Gatos, Calif., specializes in public art in general and specifically in *tromp l'oeil* — tricks on the eye — murals.

In Winslow, Pugh took a bare, brick wall and painted windows, including one with the reflection of a striking girl in a flatbed Ford, apparently slowing down to take a look at the bronze statue, which was the work of artist Ron Adamson.

For those who look closely, the license plate on the truck reads "IG7WOM" — from other lyrics in the song: I've got seven women on my mind. There's even an eagle perched on the ledge of an upstairs window.

Pugh had a blast in Winslow, spending a month there to complete the mural.

The place, still undergoing renovation, has an artsy feel, but also a homey one.

"It was like being in Mayberry," he said. "Everybody came out and brought food over. Everyone's so friendly."

The Howeths think the same thing. They moved to Winslow just about the time "Take It Easy" was on the radio in 1972. They liked the song right from the start and so did the people of Winslow. They like it even better now.

The committee would like to extend the mural the length of the bare wall. Pugh has already drawn up the plans. It's simply a matter of money. Most of the funds are being raised through the sale of bricks, engraved with donors' names, which committee members hope one day will cover the entire park. So far, more than 1,500 bricks have been sold.

People stop every day to stand on *The Corner* and have their pictures taken. People like the foursome from Phoenix who showed up the morning we were there, or the man from Belgium who also came by. People like us.

The kids rode their new scooters to *The Corner* from La Posada. As Eagles music — including "Take It Easy" — played from speakers perched in a second-floor window of a Route 66 souvenir shop across Kinsley, we snapped photos of each other, ensuring we will always remember our visit to *The Corner* whenever we hear the song.

Silly, maybe, but such a fine sight to see.

L&M's Eagles Fastlane (http://www.eaglesfans.com)
Don Henley (http://www.donhenley.com)
Standin' on the Corner Park (http://www.winslowarizona.com/)
Take it Easy (http://www.illusion-art.com/winslow/music.html)
La Posada (http://www.laposada.org/)
John Pugh, Master of Tromp L'oeil Murals (http://www.illusion-art.com)

People stop every day to stand on The Corner and have their pictures taken. People like the foursome from Phoenix ... or the man from Belgium who also came by. People like us.

Sante Fe saved us as plans unraveled

SANTA FE, N.M. — For such a long, complicated, fast-paced cross-country trip, we sure took a big gamble by having a lousy travel agent.

Me.

Despite that, for five weeks we had remarkably good fortune with our destinations and accommodations. Our plans worked out miraculously well.

But I knew my luck eventually would run out.

Somewhere between Winslow, Arizona, and Mesa Verde National Park in southwest Colorado, it did.

Thank goodness for Santa Fe. I'll get to that in a minute.

Before Santa Fe, the road got rough for us. In the course of two days, we drove hundreds of miles on back roads, saw almost nothing we'd hoped to and stayed in probably the worst motel of the trip. Along the way, I made a number of tactical mistakes: reached destinations too late, couldn't find a decent place to eat, and, in my haste, bypassed sites we should have stopped and visited. Everything seemed to go wrong.

If you've ever led a long excursion, perhaps you know the feeling: bad timing and bad vibes. It was an uncomfortable, frustrating time as the passengers began to mutiny. Under constant use, our atlas had crumbled into a half-dozen pieces during the course of the trip, and my nerves were in about the same shape.

You could almost say our plans for those two days went up in flames. In fact, an orange glow was right before our eyes as we drove through the night in northeast Arizona. At the time, we didn't know what it was. We learned later it was Mesa Verde National Park.

Mesa Verde, home of ancient cliff dwellings, was one of our destinations. Robin, Melissa and I visited there eight years ago during a trip to Colorado. It was a fascinating place we wanted to see again and introduce to Alex and Jack.

Wildfires there in July had put our visit in jeopardy, but they were finally brought under control and the park reopened — the day we were scheduled to arrive. I called the park that afternoon from Winslow, to check on a tour for the next morning. The park was busy, the woman on the phone said. Get here early.

Under constant use, our atlas had crumbled into a half-dozen pieces during the course of the trip, and my nerves were in about the same shape.

We stopped at Petrified Forest National Park in the Painted Desert of eastern Arizona, one of those freakish places where nature has played a marvelous trick, turning acres of fallen trees into rainbow-hued petrified wood.

Things turned grim after that. Darkness fell as we traveled through Indian reservations on our way to Mesa Verde. We arrived too late at the Four Corners — the only point in the country where four states meet and one of the places Alex was looking forward to seeing. The place was closed, but we stopped and snapped her photograph in the dark in front of the locked gate. It was a pretty low moment for me.

And there was that orange, smoky glow we kept seeing on the horizon. For 50 miles we saw it, not realizing a new fire had erupted at Mesa Verde since I had called that afternoon. When we arrived at our motel in nearby Cortez, Colo., the lobby was full of people who had been evacuated from the park.

"This one's really bad," the motel desk clerk told me as I checked in. "They don't know if there will even be a park left tomorrow."

In Cortez, a small place that depends on Mesa Verde as its lifeblood, this was a glum time.

With Mesa Verde closed the next day, we visited the nearby Anasazi Heritage Center in Dolores. It was a nice little museum that also featured Hopi dancers, who had been scheduled to perform at Mesa Verde that weekend. We thought about picnicking near ancient ruins along a path at the center, until we saw signs warning about rattlesnakes and mountain lions.

Thanks, we'll eat in the van.

Then it was back on the road for a long drive to Taos in the mountains of northern New Mexico. Along the way, we saw the billowing smoke of two more forest fires. We've been dodging wildfires across the West for the last few weeks. We just missed fires in Montana and Idaho and drove through the smoky haze of a Southern California fire on the way to Death Valley.

Our accommodations in Taos were nothing special and neither were our moods. Still, we enjoyed visits to the Kit Carson Home and Museum, and the Martinez Hacienda, which is thought to be the only restored hacienda opened to the public. The fortress-like house was built in 1804 and contains exhibits of Spanish colonial life.

Our spirits really lifted after making the 75-mile drive to Santa Fe.

It's amazing how roaming through an outdoor market can improve your disposition.

It's amazing how roaming through an outdoor market can improve your disposition.

An Original *Web*Pointers™ Interactive Internet Guide

On summer weekends, the Plaza in downtown Santa Fe is transformed into a marketplace of potters, jewelers and other artisans peddling their wares. After a blue corn enchilada at a downtown restaurant, we spent the afternoon wandering the Plaza, admiring the merchandise and chatting with the people who had their goods laid out in little stalls or on blankets on the sidewalk.

We bought a pretty bowl from an older Native American woman. I turned it over to find a price, but found only an "L" and a "T."

"Those are my initials," Lucy Toya said proudly.

She'd made it.

Santa Fe, an historic and eccentric city, represents a melding of Native American, Hispanic and Anglo cultures. It also seems like a big art gallery. There are paintings and sculptures everywhere. We strolled into an old mission, Santuario de Guadalupe, and found an art exhibit. While there, we also lit a candle for the rest of our journey, figuring we could use all the help we could get.

We stayed at La Fonda, an historic hotel dubbed "the inn at the end" of the Santa Fe Trail, known for its pueblo-style architecture and decor, including thick wooden beams, carved corbels and handcrafted chandeliers. Its hallways are filled with paintings, carvings and other works by local artisans, its lobby filled with local artisans — and everyone else. World War II journalist Ernie Pyle wrote, "You never met anybody anywhere except at La Fonda."

From the window of our hotel room, we could see the Loretto Chapel, which features a spiral staircase leading from the sanctuary to the choir loft that, without any supports, defies engineering logic. There's also a story behind the staircase involving the mysterious carpenter who showed up unexpectedly, built it with simple tools and then vanished without payment. Nuns were certain he was the answer to their prayers. At the very least, he was an amazingly skilled craftsman — or really lucky.

Besides art galleries, museums and old churches, Santa Fe is filled with little shops and good places to eat. So, where did our children decide they wanted to dine when we went for an early-evening walk? Why, the Five & Dime across from the Plaza, where they ordered a soft pretzel (Jack), a corn dog (Alex) and a small, frozen pizza (Melissa). At least they didn't order the — I'm quoting from the menu here — "famous Frito pie" that was on the menu.

In order to show I'm not a completely useless parent, I'd like to point out that Jack earlier had enjoyed a roasted ear of corn as we shopped on the Plaza. However, I refuse to disclose what Alex

In order to show I'm not a completely useless parent, I'd like to point out that Jack earlier had enjoyed a roasted ear of corn as we shopped on the Plaza.

and Melissa had eaten previously that day, but I don't believe a vegetable had crossed their lips.

At that point, though, I really didn't care who ate what. I was just happy we were entering the home stretch of our trip in a good frame of mind.

Thanks, Santa Fe.

Mesa Verde National Park (http://www.nps.gov/meve/)
Petrified Forest National Park (http://www.nps.gov/pefo/)
Anasazi Heritage Center (http://www.swcolo.org/Tourism/Archaeology/AnasaziHeritageCenter.html)
Kit Carson Home and Museum (http://taosvacationguide.com/MAT/kit.html)
Martinez Hacienda (http://www.laplaza.org/art/museums_mtz.php3)
La Fonda Hotel (http://www.santafe.org/lafonda/index.html)
Loretto Chapel (http://www.lorettochapel.com/html/stair.html)
Santa Fe Convention and Visitors Bureau (http://www.santafe.org)

I was just happy we were entering the home stretch of our trip in a good frame of mind.

A slight jaunt south of the border

EL PASO, Texas — God bless America.

We were only gone for a few hours, but, my goodness, it was good to get back on U.S. soil.

No wonder there's a border problem with Mexico. I'd be trying to get out of there, too.

During our stay in El Paso, we ventured into Juarez, Mexico, the city on the opposite side of the Rio Grande. We parked Big Blue and walked across a bridge.

It was a sweaty stroll into another world.

Maybe Juarez is not representative of Mexico and maybe the parts of Juarez we saw are not representative of Juarez, but from what we could see I came away with a clear conclusion: what a sad, miserable place.

But you can see that without actually entering Juarez. Drive along Interstate 10 as it hugs the Rio Grande through El Paso and you see a hillside littered with dilapidated houses and unpaved roads. That would be Juarez.

This was a real eye-opener — or at least I hope it was — for our children.

Nothing much is required to enter Juarez. No passport, no birth certificate, no proof of citizenship — just three pesos (25 cents) apiece to walk across the Santa Fe Street Bridge, one of the bridges that link El Paso and Juarez. (To travel deeper into Mexico requires more formal paperwork.)

Trolleys run regularly between El Paso and Juarez, hauling tourists here and there, but we decided to walk.

We entered Juarez armed with a map, a jug of ice water and a rising eighth-grader who is entering her third year of Spanish.

Earlier in the trip we'd listened to a compact disc that promised we would learn Spanish while we drove. Listening got a little tedious and we didn't end up learning much more than how to ask for the train to Madrid, which didn't do us a whole lot of good.

What I really needed to learn to say in Spanish was "Please, don't bother me anymore."

As you know, all Americans are extremely rich, so we were obvious targets. We weren't a block off the bridge when a man sitting on a street corner in front of a shop said, "Can I help you spend your money?"

This was a real eye-opener — or at least I hope it was — for our children.

A hand-written advertisement for Viagra was tacked to the outside wall of a store. Stray dogs roamed the streets.

As we walked through Juarez, we were accosted by beggars and people selling just about anything — dolls, ice cream, information. This was not unexpected, but after about the fifth wave it became a little overwhelming.

The hustling merchants in the stalls at the City Market — a place frequented by tourists — were really something. I'm sure some people thrive on what I'll charitably call this "interaction." But I consider it harassment and it turns me off like a light switch.

They watched us everywhere we went; it felt like surveillance. They touched our arms, blocked our way, greeted us at every turn inside the market. Never threatening, always nice, forever smiling. But very, very persistent.

Everyone called me *amigo*. One guy told me he was offering "special prices today" (there were, of course, no price tags on anything). Another named Joe, apparently my best friend in Juarez, shook my hand and insisted I sit down at his outdoor cafe.

They were very polite, but it wore me out.

After a little browsing, we huddled together and Robin asked what we wanted to get.

I offered, "How about 'out'?"

We bought a few things, but saw a lot more: old women with earnest eyes begging on street corners with Styrofoam cups; a fellow on the bridge to El Paso playing his accordion while his dirty, barefoot children played nearby, traffic whizzing past.

The streets of Juarez were full of potholes. The buildings all needed a good coat of paint. Lots of people seemed to need something to do.

Melissa translated signs for us. Jack banged on the bongos we bought him. Alex asked, "When are we going back to America?"

As we were leaving the City Market, a hulking pink building covered with graffiti and peeling paint, an older woman wearing a shawl and selling little birds made of yarn approached us. We politely declined her offer, but the birds, naturally, caught the kids' eyes. Each wanted one. Two bucks apiece. We could have done worse, I guess. Maybe it made her day.

By the time we got back to El Paso — I didn't kiss the ground, but I felt like it — it was mid-afternoon, so we stopped for lunch at a place that served Mexican food and also provided the

Alex asked, "When are we going back to America?"

funniest scene of the day. While we were eating, a pizza-delivery guy showed up at the front counter of the restaurant with a couple of pizzas. For the employees.

After lunch, we took a drive around town.

The Rio Grande is El Paso's natural boundary to the south, while mountains are wedged into the middle of the city. There are lots of rocks and dirt, a few palms and cactus. We drove along Scenic Drive, a high, winding road that provided an exquisite view of El Paso and, of course, Juarez and Mexico beyond.

One thing we noticed about El Paso and, for that matter, New Mexico is that many houses are surrounded by stone walls. Nice walls and all sizes of houses. Sometimes it seemed likely the walls cost more than the houses. Reminds you of the haciendas, which were built in this part of the country generations ago to provide fortress-like protection.

The Hispanic influence in El Paso is obviously very strong. Late one evening, I had to visit a Target to buy a few odds and ends (OK, we shipped many of our dirty clothes home to make more room in the van, we didn't sort those clothes very well before we mailed them, and some of us ran out of undergarments). The closing announcement on the loudspeaker was given in English and Spanish. The English must have been solely for my benefit because everyone I heard at the check-out registers — employees and customers — was speaking Spanish.

Our driving tour of El Paso ended on the east side of town in the suburb of Ysleta, the oldest settlement in Texas. We stopped at Mission Ysleta, an old adobe church built more than 300 years ago.

We ducked into the church, sitting for a while in the wooden pews, admiring the tall, narrow sanctuary, the paintings on the walls and the ornate altar. Parishioners began arriving for an evening service. There they stood in the doorway. I heard the mission bell.

We were there only a few minutes, but the quiet of the mission provided a good place to contemplate what we had seen earlier in the day and to give thanks for what we have.

El Paso, TX (http://www.ci.el-paso.tx.us)
Mission Ysleta (http://elpasoparishes.org/MisHisYsleta.htm)
El Paso Convention & Visitors Bureau (http://www.elpasocvb.com)

We were there only a few minutes, but the quiet of the mission provided a good place to contemplate what we had seen earlier in the day and to give thanks for what we have.

Remember the Alamo ... and the whales

SAN ANTONIO, Texas — So there we were, eating our chicken-fried steak and Gulf shrimp more than 500 feet above the ground. And spinning.

The entire restaurant atop the Tower of the Americas, the centerpiece of the 1968 World's Fair, rotates very slowly, meaning if you eat deliberately enough you can nibble your nachos overlooking the Alamo and your vanilla ice cream as you peer down at the Alamodome.

This is assuming, of course, the rotation does not cause you to lose your nachos or ice cream.

The more fortunate part of lunch on this spinning top is that the restaurant is completely surrounded by glass — so no spilled milk, stray fries or errant forks from our table actually threatened those walking on the ground far below.

This was not our best lunch of the trip, but it surely was the lunch that offered the greatest perspective.

Which sort of sums up San Antonio for us: it may not have been our best stop, but it was close. We did a little bit of everything, and we left here completely worn out after two extremely full days.

... it has a big pool. When you're traveling with three kids the reasons you choose certain accommodations do not have to be consistently high-brow.

San Antonio is a relentlessly hospitable city with a range of attractions, from solemn history to killer whales splashing tourists with their tails.

We arrived in San Antonio after a bearish, 550-mile drive from El Paso. You know it looking at the map, but it's still stunning to me that you can drive more than 500 miles and travel little more than halfway across Texas. We broke up the trip with a number of stops, including a swim in a huge, spring-fed pool — containing actual fish — at Balmorehea State Park, which is not far off Interstate 10 but just east of nowhere, and a visit to Ozona — the self-proclaimed "best little town in the world" — where a monument to David Crockett anchors the town square.

In San Antonio, we stayed downtown at the Menger Hotel, which was perfect for us because it is steeped in history, it resides across the street from the Alamo and it has a big pool. When you're traveling with three kids the reasons you choose certain accommodations do not have to be consistently high-brow.

The Menger opened in 1859 and has the stories to prove it. Gen. Robert E. Lee once rode his horse into the lobby, scooped up the toddler daughter of the Menger family and presented her with a gold locket; Gen. Ulysses S. Grant drained a few glasses in the Menger Bar. At the same bar, Teddy Roosevelt recruited his "rough riders." It is a hotel with a Lee Room and a Grant Room and a Minuet Room. A pianist plays in the lobby. It's a nice place. They let us stay anyway.

Before leaving Richmond, we'd read a number of books about places we'd see along the way. One of the places that really interested Alex, a rising first-grader, was the Alamo. She was fascinated by the stories of David Crockett and James Bowie and the line in the sand.

The Alamo itself is not quite like anything I've ever visited. Little of the original structure still stands, but it doesn't much matter. There is a reverence associated with the place — and the people who work there — that gives it the feel of a church, which the Alamo, a Spanish mission, actually was in the beginning.

Texans, of course, hold this as hallowed ground. Though the scene of a losing battle, the Alamo was the launching pad for Texas independence.

Consider the sign at the entrance to the Alamo shrine

Quiet

No Smoking

Gentlemen

Remove Hats

No Pictures

No Refreshments

Contributing to the sanctity of the place is the fact there is no admission charge. The Alamo is run by the Daughters of the Republic of Texas and has been since 1905. Before that, the Alamo had changed hands a number of times and, at one point, was a store.

These days, money to operate the Alamo comes from donations and proceeds from the sale of Davy Crockett coonskin caps and Jim Bowie knives at the Alamo gift shop.

Because the Alamo was so close to the Menger and because it cost nothing to go in, we stopped by the Alamo three times — for short visits and walks among the shade trees and immaculate gardens. The property is not particularly large, so there is not much to view, but there is a lot to consider. You come away with the sense you have just left a sacred place.

Outside the Alamo, the best way to see the sights in San Antonio is through its mass transit

Texans, of course, hold this as hallowed ground. Though the scene of a losing battle, the Alamo was the launching pad for Texas independence.

It featured considerable general information but also some very personal stories — such as the Texas Jewish family who used the rowels on their spurs to make the holes in the traditional matzo.

system. We rode a trolley across town for 50 cents apiece when we visited Market Square, where we wandered through a Mexican market and ate dinner at Mi Tierra Cafe & Bakery, a Tex-Mex restaurant that is a San Antonio institution, serving up equal measures of good food and colorful atmosphere.

We also took a Texas Trolley Tour, which introduced us to a number of historic sites around town. Among our stops was Mission San Jose, the largest of San Antonio's four missions, where we strolled the grounds and watched a fabulous movie that put into perspective San Antonio's past, specifically how the Spaniards and their missions changed the culture of Native Americans and the course of history.

We visited San Fernando Cathedral, the oldest cathedral sanctuary in the nation and the place where the ashes of all but one of the Alamo defenders are entombed.

And we stopped by the Institute of Texan Cultures, which focuses on the contributions of 27 ethnic groups that settled Texas. It featured considerable general information but also some very personal stories — such as the Texas Jewish family who used the rowels on their spurs to make the holes in the traditional matzo.

We spent an evening on the city's ballyhooed River Walk, the highlight being a slow boat tour along the river, which is more of a glorified ditch than a river as it winds through downtown. But this is some ditch: with cafes and hotels and upscale malls along its banks.

River Walk is a nice place but hardly new. It's almost 60 years old, but for years it was such an undesirable place that even locals — much less tourists — feared visiting.

But HemisFair, the 1968 World's Fair, changed the complexion of everything in San Antonio. City leaders got serious about tourism and River Walk, now famous and thriving, is one of the most tangible results.

San Antonio is a good travel destination for families because of its variety of offerings and the ease with which you can get around town. All of this is fine and good for parents, but the kids want to see the whales.

So we took our three to Sea World of Texas, which had been a nice prize we'd held out the entire trip. The day we visited also happened to be Melissa's 13th birthday, so the timing was excellent.

We rode rides, we ate amusement park food and we watched a number of shows involving dolphins and other critters. We saw an otter speak into a microphone and then dive into a toilet. It's too involved to explain.

But the highlight, the absolute highlight for Alex and Melissa was getting splashed by Shamu — or one of the other killer whales that made Sea World famous. (I can't tell them apart.) I don't think Alex and Melissa will ever want to wash those clothes again. But then, we've got a lot of other clothes like that, too.

The rest of us sat a few rows higher, less enthusiastic about cold, salt water flying all over us.

For getting wet, I prefer the hotel pool, and the Menger's was just right: tables with umbrellas, thick, warm towels and no whales.

Tower of the Americas (http://www.toweroftheamericas.com)
The Alamo (http://www.thealamo.org)
Balmorehea State Park (http://www.geocities.com/pipeline/ramp/8975/html/texdivesites.html)
Menger Hotel (http://www.historicmenger.com)
Daughters of the Republic of Texas (http://www.drtl.org/drt_info.html)
Mi Tierra Cafe & Bakery (http://sanantonio.citysearch.com/E/V/SATTX/0001/54/53)
Mission San Jose (http://www.nps.gov/saan/saanjo01.htm)
San Fernando Cathedral (http://www.sfcathedral.org)
Institute of Texan Cultures (http://www.texancultures.utsa.edu/main)
River Walk (http://www.stic.net/users/sarwt)
Sea World (http://www.seaworld.com)
San Antonio Convention & Visitors Bureau (http://www.sanantoniocvb.com)

But the highlight, the absolute highlight for Alex and Melissa was getting splashed by Shamu — or one of the other killer whales that made Sea World famous. (I can't tell them apart.)

The Big Easy welcomes weary travelers

NEW ORLEANS — Privacy is hard to come by on a cross-country trip with three kids.

We've traveled more than 8,000 miles in a van. We've grown close. Very close. Too close, it seems sometimes.

We've slept in a single tent. We've slept mostly in single motel rooms with two beds and space on the floor for at least one sleeping bag.

We've gone almost everywhere together. With our kids 13, 6 and 3, it's not like you can send them off on their own exploring.

There's no escape.

Which is why you take solitude where you can get it. Like the gas station bathroom in New Mexico. As rooms go, it was not particularly nice. As gas station bathrooms go, it was not particularly nice. But it was quiet. And I was alone. I lingered. I pressed the button on the automatic hand-dryer a second time.

Which brings me to New Orleans. In our attempt to stay in a variety of places on our trip, we booked a room at the Hotel Inter-Continental, easily the fanciest hotel on our itinerary. It's the sort of place where there's not only a telephone in the bathroom but a television. In addition, the hotel provided us two rooms, joined by a door. The kids stayed in one room, Robin and I stayed in the other. Everyone had a bed. Everyone got chocolates on their pillows.

New Orleans: home of jazz, gumbo and connecting hotel rooms.

My kind of town.

We made a somewhat inauspicious arrival in New Orleans, showing up around midnight after a 500-mile drive from San Antonio. The kids were asleep, and all of us were rather scraggly looking when we pulled Big Blue up to the hotel's swanky entrance.

A bellhop greeted us, perhaps alarmed that we were about to become actual guests. I waved off valet parking, told him I'd park it myself later and went inside to register. Meanwhile, Robin woke the kids, and had them gather their belongings and pile them outside the van. So, awaiting my return, there they stood : bed-headed and bedraggled, a motley crew with stuffed animals, pillow buddies and suitcases. Alex climbed atop our mountain of belongings and went back to sleep. Everyone else just looked dazed and disturbed.

New Orleans: home of jazz, gumbo and connecting hotel rooms. ... My kind of town.

About this time, the limos started rolling in and out stepped women in slinky black evening gowns and men dressed in suits, all of whom eyed my wife and children suspiciously. Robin, desperately wishing she could sink into the pavement and extremely glad we don't know anyone in New Orleans, said the well-heeled arrivals stepped gingerly around the pile of Lohmanns as they headed into the hotel, not knowing, I'm sure, whether to feel pity or concern.

We just felt tired.

Much refreshed the next day, we set out to see New Orleans.

New Orleans, of course, is a fine place for fun-loving adults. We also found plenty of good, appropriate stuff to do with the kids. Walking down Bourbon Street wasn't one of them, although we did it anyway.

We roamed around the French Quarter, admiring the French and Spanish architecture — and the smell of the previous night's spilled beer. But that's New Orleans. It is at once graceful, exquisite and earthy. One storefront advertises the best muffulettas in town; the next topless *and* bottomless.

As long as you expect variety, you will do fine here.

We roamed through the French market, brimming with food, produce and souvenirs. We bought postcards and bananas, then sat down and ate the latter as a snack on a French Quarter bench.

For our real meals on our one full day in New Orleans, we ate crawfish cakes, jambalaya, red bean soup and other fine local fare at two little cafes we just happened by in the French Quarter. For supper, Alex ordered scrambled eggs and bacon. She was quite proud of her unorthodox selection until I mentioned it came with grits. She does not typically encounter grits.

"What's that?" she asked, wrinkling up her nose, when her plate arrived.

I ate the grits.

In Jackson Square, the heart of the Quarter, just across the street from the Mississippi riverfront, we encountered a guy making balloon animals, an old man strumming a red guitar and singing, and a large fellow sharing a park bench with his tuba. One character had himself all chained up and was writhing on the ground trying to get loose; passersby stopped to watch and one onlooker dropped a dollar into his box, figuring, I guess, a little incentive might help. A few feet away, a service was under way in St. Louis Cathedral.

New Orleans: everything, all the time.

It is at once graceful, exquisite and earthy. One storefront advertises the best muffulettas in town; the next topless and bottomless.

Around the corner, a young artist offered to sketch your portrait for five dollars. "Ugly people," his sign read, "$1 extra."

We visited Aquarium of the Americas, on the banks of the Mississippi, and we saw sea horses, sea otters and a white alligator. The kids touched a shark. I did them one better the next day when we took a swamp tour and I held an alligator in my bare hands. I'll let you ponder that image for a moment and will return to the swamp shortly.

We rode the St. Charles Avenue streetcar line. The vintage 1920s streetcars took us through the Garden District of New Orleans, which features mansions and lovely gardens but also numerous neighborhoods. It was an instructive ride — also pleasantly cool with the old, wood-framed windows wide open — in that it's easy to forget while cavorting in the Quarter that people actually live in New Orleans.

Proving there's more to New Orleans than beignets and good, strong coffee, we ventured up Interstate 10 on our way out of town and got off at Bayou Sauvage National Wildlife Refuge. It's a swamp.

We bought a ticket for a boat ride offered by New Orleans Swamp Tours. There are numerous swamp tours in southern Louisiana. This one just happened to be most convenient for us, since the wildlife refuge is a little east of the city, which was the direction we were headed.

On board, our captain and guide, Joey Hatty, a knowledgable, entertaining sort, explained to us that if the boat were to sink, we should not worry; the canal we were traveling was only a few feet deep. However, if we really wanted to panic and put on a life jacket, we were welcome to. We just needed to consider that the favorite color of alligators is orange, which happened to be the color of the life jackets. We also were welcome to run screaming to the nearest shore, but, he said, we would likely encounter the fiercest of all swamp creatures: not gators or water moccasins or the frighteningly ugly garfish that patrol the waters.

No, the most feared swamp creature in these parts, Joey said, is the Louisiana mosquito.

Thank goodness, the boat did not sink.

During the two-hour tour, we saw numerous gators from a distance, along with egrets and heron. The closest we got to a gator, however, came on board. Joey, who used to trap gators and is now a commercial fisherman and substitute schoolteacher, rescued a baby gator a while back. It's now less than a year old and about a foot long.

I did them one better the next day when we took a swamp tour and I held an alligator.

Meantime, he plays show-and-tell with it for his tour guests. I held the gator for a while, so all the kids could pet it.

Hatty plans to release it into the wild in about six months when it can better fend for itself. I'd say that's a good plan since any wild animal that would let me hold it probably is not that wild and needs a little more seasoning.

Hatty, who has Cajun roots, grew up in the area and still lives there, was full of information and stories. Years ago, when he was a kid, before alligators were deemed endangered, a license to hunt gators cost a buck-fifty. When Joey was 14, his father let him go off on his own to hunt gators for the first time. He and a buddy shot 10 that day, sold the hides and made a bundle, almost $3,000 apiece.

We reminded Melissa she turns 14 next year.

The best piece of information from Joey came at the end of the tour. He recommended a little seafood restaurant back up the road a few miles. Locals love it, he said.

We did, too. Lama's, it was called, a combination seafood market and restaurant, just east of New Orleans. Didn't look like much from the outside. Inside, though, the boiled shrimp were just about the best we'd ever tasted. The gumbo was great, and the soft-shell crabs weren't bad either.

Only thing missing was a nice, cozy table for two. But we don't need one of those on this trip.

Hotel Inter-Continental (http://www.neworleanshotel.com/promotions.html)
Bayou Sauvage National Wildlife Refuge (http://southeastlouisiana.fws.gov/bsed.html)
New Orleans Swamp Tours (http://southeastlouisiana.fws.gov/bsed.html)
Lama's Seafood Restaurant and Market (http://www.fishing-boating.com/lamas/)
New Orleans Convention & Visitors Bureau (http://www.neworleanscvb.com)

Inside, though, the boiled shrimp were just about the best we'd ever tasted. The gumbo was great, and the soft-shell crabs weren't bad either.

Hotel (with a/c) saves intrepid campers

PENSACOLA BEACH, Fla. — Here's a mistake:

Camping on the Florida Panhandle in August, with three kids, at the end of a very long trip.

I'm not sure what possessed us to schedule this, but we did.

It proved to be a night to remember.

But only because there's no way we can forget it.

We showed up late at Gulf Islands National Seashore after a drive along the Gulf coast from New Orleans. We had to fumble in the dark to pitch our tent. The kids were hungry and cranky. It was sweltering.

Maybe we've got the wrong kind of tent, maybe it's some sort of tent made for camping in Alaska. I don't know, but even with the vents open it held the heat like a double-boiler. I felt like a poached egg.

Alex was squirming and fussing, unable to get comfortable. Jack was flopping around on the sleeping bags like a crazed mackerel. Melissa was shrieking, but only when the raccoon came by to sniff us. She mostly kept her cool when she nearly rubbed noses with a skunk that pressed its nose against the screen of our tent. And she didn't even see the armadillo that Robin spotted through the opening on the other side.

It was like Wild Kingdom, although I'm not sure who was watching whom.

I awoke after what seemed like 10 or 12 hours of fitful sleep, half of which I was certain must have been some sort of ritualized torture. Robin was already awake.

"What time is it?" she asked in a hollow tone, clearly hoping I was going to say "Tomorrow."

I looked at my watch. A quarter after midnight.

The night seemed as if it would not end.

Finally, mercifully, it did.

At which point, I went looking for a hotel, lucking into one at a deep discount — Florida schools were already back in session and the beachfront Hampton Inn had rooms to fill — on Pensacola Beach. The emerald Gulf waters lapped up on the sugar white beach, just beyond the beckoning hotel pools. The people were friendly, the air conditioning worked flawlessly.

Alex was squirming and fussing, unable to get comfortable. Jack was flopping around on the sleeping bags like a crazed mackerel. Melissa was shrieking, ...

The children cheered me when I reported back following my successful mission.

It has been uncanny on this trip how good, without fail, has always chased bad.

Every time I've been ready to throw in the towel — and the sleeping bags, the maps and the laptop — something unexpectedly positive has happened to rescue us.

This time the hotel — a Hampton Inn — and the beach saved us.

There are a number of interesting things to do around Pensacola: the National Museum of Naval Aviation, Fort Pickens, historic Pensacola Village, museums, a zoo. We didn't do any of them. This was really the first time since we left Richmond that we had the opportunity to catch our breath. And that's exactly what we did.

For three full days, we did little more than play on the beach, play in the Gulf and play in the pool. It was great.

We even established a family tradition: dinner at Peg Leg Pete's Oyster Bar. We ate dinner there three nights in a row. I can't say with any range of authority that Peg Leg Pete's has the best food on the beach, but we liked it. The service was genuinely nice, the seafood was fresh and varied, the menu included 20 beers on tap, and the kids' meals came in green plastic sand buckets that you take with you when you leave. Can't beat that with a sand shovel.

I'd learned of Peg Leg Pete's on my mission to find a hotel. My mission that fateful morning also had included finding a telephone line from which I could transmit an article from my laptop to the Times-Dispatch.

The campground offered no phone lines. A National Park Service ranger suggested a public library in nearby Gulf Breeze. No phone jacks. After leaving the library, however, I saw a small business that advertised itself as handling faxes, copies and shipping. I walked in and asked if I could pay to use a phone jack. The proprietor said, no, I couldn't pay but I was most welcome to use her phone. Before departing, I asked for a restaurant recommendation. Without hesitation, she suggested Peg Leg Pete's.

I thank her.

We played miniature golf one night. Alex got a hole-in-one. She was excited. Jack didn't get a hole-in-one, but he was excited anyway. He plays an enthusiastic game of golf. He drags more than he putts, sort of sweeping the ball into the cup. When that doesn't work, he picks up the ball in his hand and drops it in.

It has been uncanny on this trip how good, without fail, has always chased bad.

It's a simple game.

And I should say the National Seashore was a fine place. I'd like to go back sometime. Just not at the end of a long, weary trip. Maybe not in the middle of August. And quite possibly not with five of us roasting together in the same, small tent.

We enjoyed a day there on its secluded beach, which is stunningly gorgeous and peaceful.

But at this point in our trip, we craved civilization.

As we drove out of the campground on our way to the hotel, past the other campers settling in for another suffocating night, I felt somewhat guilty but also slightly smug, like a parolee leaving prison while the residents left behind still had time to serve.

Gulf Islands National Seashore (http://www.nps.gov/guis)
National Museum of Naval Aviation (http://www.naval-air.org)
Historic Pensacola Village (http://www.dos.state.fl.us/dhr/pensacola)
Fort Pickens (http://www.tulane.edu/~latner/Pickens.html)
Peg Leg Pete's Oyster Bar (http://www.peglegpetes.com/restaurant.html)
Hampton Inn Pensacola Beach (http://www.hampton-inn.com)

... at this point in our trip, we craved civilization.

Peachy reminiscences in Georgia

ATLANTA — Good fortune has followed us on our cross-country trip.

We've experienced no problems with the van, we've had no illnesses and no one in our party has been convicted of or even arraigned on felony charges.

Our remarkable good luck continued in Atlanta, where we learned upon entering Zoo Atlanta that we were invited to Aaron's birthday party.

Aaron is a giraffe. He turned 3.

Cupcakes for everyone! (Except Aaron.)

The kids certainly thought we were lucky to hit the zoo on party day, and, since I also got a cupcake, I was inclined to agree with them.

We scheduled Atlanta as the last official stop on our itinerary because it's an interesting city, but mostly because we used to live there in the 1980s.

We drove by our first house, in the Atlanta suburbs, and were thoroughly unimpressed by what the current residents have done with the place. They apparently do not own pruning shears. All of the shrubs and trees we'd lovingly planted and cared for have been allowed to go wild. So have the weeds. It was a little sad to see, but also gratifying to know the red tips are 15 feet tall.

Still, Robin pronounced seeing our old house the highlight of her trip. The kids — Melissa lived in the house until she was 7 months old and proudly considers herself an Atlanta native; Alex and Jack had never even seen the place — were interested enough to get out and watch their mother shoot photographs (while I sat in the van, praying the current residents would not arrive home while we were playing tourists in front of their house).

The children were most taken by the Big Chicken.

The Big Chicken is a large, mechanical bird — its beak clucks and its eyes roll — that towers above a KFC Restaurant in Marietta, a suburb northwest of Atlanta. It is a landmark. It is a source of pride. It also is pretty goofy.

We went inside and saw hanging on the wall a framed copy of an article I'd written about the Big Chicken maybe 15 years ago when I worked in United Press International's Atlanta bureau. The kids thought that was pretty cool. (So did I.) We bought three t-shirts and a stuffed chicken. However, we weren't much in the mood for chicken so we ate dinner elsewhere.

The kids certainly thought we were lucky to hit the zoo on party day, and, since I also got a cupcake, I was inclined to agree with them.

But the main event of our very full day in Atlanta had been Zoo Atlanta, which has accomplished a stunning turnaround in the past decade-and-a-half. In the early 1980s, the zoo was deemed one of the 10 worst in the country, not exactly the sort of distinction you print on bumper stickers.

Its facilities were poor and it suffered through one embarrassing incident after another; once, the prairie dog holes were inadvertently filled with cement. It was a laughingstock. But corporate Atlanta rallied around the zoo, raising the money that transformed an ambitious vision into national respectability. It's nice to see how far it's come. It's also a most pleasant place to spend a day.

The zoo is in Grant Park, a city park about a mile from Turner Field, home of the Atlanta Braves.

The Braves were not home the day we visited, but the giant pandas were.

I recall visiting the pandas at the National Zoo in Washington D.C. on a number of occasions and rarely seeing them active, if I even saw them. We walked into the panda exhibit at Zoo Atlanta, and there they were: one chomping bamboo in a panda hammock, the other in a nearby doorway. Before long, the two were engaged in a little king of the hill action, wrestling and playing, with one finally knocking the other on his fanny.

They were quite entertaining.

But to me, the most fascinating creatures at Zoo Atlanta are the gorillas. The Ford African Rain Forest was one of the first naturalistic habitats for gorillas. The four gorilla families who live here look far happier roaming through the trees and open grassy areas than gorillas I've seen at other zoos living behind concrete and glass.

At Zoo Atlanta, the people are behind the concrete and glass.

Zoo Atlanta is not particularly big, but it does what it does very well. It offers remarkable accessibility to the animals and much in the way of visitor satisfaction. There were lots of zoo employees and volunteers on hand the day we visited to answer questions and provide guidance. Once, I merely *looked* lost as I pulled out a map and a zoo worker approached us and asked if she could help.

After the zoo, we visited another Atlanta institution with legendary customer relations: Coca-Cola. (Remember *New* Coke and the way the company backpedaled cheerfully from that fiasco?)

Actually, we went to the World of Coca-Cola, which is sort of a museum to the drink (and company), which has had as much to do with the emergence of Atlanta as anything.

The World of Coca-Cola is full of artifacts and company history. Its mere existence — as well

Once, I merely looked lost as I pulled out a map and a zoo worker approached us and asked if she could help.

as the chutzpah to charge adults $6 admission — is evidence of the marketing genius that transformed a glass of fizz into one of the world's most powerful companies.

I particularly enjoyed watching clips of Coca-Cola's television advertising through the years. But the highlight for the kids was the tasting room at the end of the self-guided tour. Visitors can sample all of the familiar Coca-Cola products — nifty automatic dispensers give the place a space-age feel — as well as the not-so-familiar ones that are sold internationally.

There's no accounting for taste in some countries. We tried a soft drink sold in Italy that aroused our taste buds the way a household cleaner might.

After the World of Coca-Cola, it was across the street to Underground Atlanta, a strip of restaurants and shops beneath the streets of the city. It's a nice enough little district — it was dormant when we lived in Atlanta in the mid 1980s and was reborn about 10 years ago — but it pales in comparison to San Antonio's River Walk. We escaped there, buying little more than candied apples for the kids.

We walked the few blocks to Centennial Park, constructed for the 1996 Olympics. It's across the street from CNN Center in the heart of downtown. The dancing fountains are the big draw. You're welcome to run, jump or merely stand in the water and get soaked. We opted to simply get sticky. Melissa, Alex and Jack worked relentlessly on the candied apples for a good half-hour, finally determining it would be easier to simply schedule an appointment to have the dentist extract their teeth.

They may not have finished their candied apples, but I think they appreciated them. Soon enough our odyssey will be over and they will be longing for the days when they were allowed to eat cupcakes and candied apples and drink cup after cup of Coke — all within a span of six hours.

They also might miss singing "Happy Birthday" to a giraffe.

Zoo Atlanta (http://www.zooatlanta.org/splash3.html)
Big Chicken (http://www.bigchicken.com/history.html)
Atlanta Braves (http://www.atlantabraves.com)
Ford African Rain Forest (http://www.zooatlanta.org/anim_exh_farf.html)
World of Coca-Cola (http://www.roadsideamerica.com/attract/GAATLcoke.html)
Underground Atlanta (http://www.underatl.com)

Soon enough our odyssey will be over and they will be longing for the days when they were allowed to eat cupcakes and candied apples and drink cup after cup of Coke — all within a span of six hours.

Preparing for re-entry

HEADED HOME — We began our final day on the road with Melissa waking up in a motel room, gazing up from her sleeping bag and groggily asking a question that perfectly captured the closing days of our long, cross-country trip.

"Where are we?"

We were in Commerce, Ga., an hour outside Atlanta. We'd spent the previous day in Atlanta, eaten a late dinner and headed north. Toward home.

The kids fell asleep soon after Spaghetti Junction, the interstate interchange where I-85 and I-285 and all their affiliated ramps and overpasses converge pasta-like northeast of Atlanta. I kept driving. They didn't know we were in Commerce, didn't really know where Commerce was.

They only knew we were on the way home to sleep in our own beds.

Jack and Alex already were planning to introduce the new stuffed animals (and toy tractors) they've purchased on vacation to their old ones waiting in their rooms at home. Melissa was making plans to call her friends. Robin was wondering what it would be like to return to the daily routine of life at home and at work.

I just wanted to sleep. And wash clothes.

I hoped our washing machine enjoyed its time off because we were about to use it within an inch of its life for the next few days.

It's funny, after seven weeks on the road, after such an excellent adventure, we were eager to get home, yet reluctant to resume our normal lives. I felt a little like one of those astronauts back in the 1960s, whose exploits in space had been witnessed back home but was now coming back to earth, about to splash down into the rest of his life. If you're not careful, you can burn up on re-entry, you know?

We did not race home the last day, stopping in South Carolina to buy a basket of fresh peaches and then pulling off the road one exit later to eat a few of them under the Peachoid, a water tower painted to look like a giant peach in Gaffney.

After our peach snack, we dallied further, driving across the highway to a new outlet mall and doing some back-to-school shopping. We didn't start home again until nearly dinnertime. It was almost as if we were delaying the inevitable.

I hoped our washing machine enjoyed its time off because we were about to use it within an inch of its life for the next few days.

An Original *WebPointers*™ Interactive Internet Guide

Robin drove most of the way home, so I could ride shotgun and write on my laptop. We took a dinner break in Durham, N.C., eating chicken, biscuits, baked beans, and macaroni and cheese. It was 9 o'clock and we were still 150 miles from home, but when you've traveled almost 10,000 miles in less than two months, that's a spin around the corner.

After dinner, I was tired of writing so I went back to driving. I shoved Simon and Garfunkel's "Homeward Bound" into the CD player — and promptly got on I-85 going the wrong way. An exit later, we had 154 miles to go.

(Robin insisted I point out that she drove more than 300 miles on the last leg of our journey, all in the right direction.)

When we pulled into our driveway just before midnight, the kids were asleep. Alex and Jack required rides to bed; Melissa, now a teenager, was on her own.

The house looked different, although strangely familiar. It's amazing how seven weeks away from a place can blur your memory.

My mother and sister had stocked our refrigerator with food for breakfast the next morning. Our neighbors had left us a loaf of homemade zucchini bread in the kitchen and a hand-painted "Welcome Home" sign in the sun room.

Upstairs we found baskets of clothes, which we recognized as those we shipped home dirty from the road. My mother had washed them and left notes on each basket marked "clean." In our house, you can never be too sure.

Robin and I started going through the mountains of mail and newspapers. We poured cold drinks. It was nice to get ice from our refrigerator instead of a convenience store.

The van needed unpacking and cleaning, clothes needed washing and putting away. We had stuff — so much stuff — everywhere. The trip allowed us to put our lives on hold, but life itself did not pause while we were gallivanting around the country. Now, we must sprint to catch up. Soccer practice is under way, the first day of school is coming up. Summer is almost gone.

It's all a little overwhelming. We did not know quite what to do first. But there was no question where we were — or where we belonged.

Home.

The Peachoid (http://www.roadsideamerica.com/attract/SCGAFpeach.html)

I went back to driving ... and promptly got on I-85 going the wrong way. An exit later, we had 154 miles to go.

We ate well most all the time

We knew it was going to be difficult eating nutritiously while traveling cross-country this summer. I don't believe, however, we could have envisioned dining on doughnuts for dinner in Cody, Wyo.

We're not necessarily proud of that, but, in simplest terms, you eat what you got.

And doughnuts were what we had that night when we returned to our motel room after an evening at a rodeo, where we barely arrived on time because we'd been driving all day.

Did I mention it was 10:30 p.m. MDT when we ate those doughnuts for dinner?

So, that's a bad example. Overall, I think we did fairly well food-wise, given constraints of time, money and availability, even if, while driving through South Dakota, Jack and Alex were poking through the food bag and excitedly asked if they could have a Flintstones vitamin as a snack.

Sure. Have two.

The key to our eating during the first half of our trip was having a large cooler between the front seats in the conversion van. In it, we kept bottles of water, soft drinks, orange juice, milk for Jack (no one else in our family is a milk-drinker), fruit and carrots, grape jelly and, on occasion, deli stuff. We ate when and where we needed to. It wasn't fancy, but the food was readily available and far cheaper — and the dining less time-consuming — than stopping for a prepared meal. We just had to remember to buy ice every once in a while.

After reaching the Pacific coast and turning, we continued to stock the cooler but we picnicked less and ate in restaurants more. Part of that was because of the heat and the landscape; in New Mexico, one rest stop was built on stilts and featured prominent signs warning about rattlesnakes. Part of it also was because we were entering areas of the country — the Southwest, the Gulf Coast — where we were eager to sample regional dishes.

But part of it also, I think, was because we were becoming tired and maybe a little lazy. It became easier to plop down in a restaurant and have someone else bring our food.

Breakfast, however, didn't change throughout the trip. We usually kept a supply of doughnuts or bagels in the van, along with a variety of cereals and fruit. We often stayed in motels or hotels that provided free continental breakfasts. Some motels provided little more than toast and coffee; others, though, offered a vast array of pastries, cold and hot cereals, yogurt, juices, milk and coffee.

... Jack and Alex were poking through the food bag and excitedly asked if they could have a Flintstones vitamin as a snack. Sure. Have two.

Otherwise, we ventured out for beignets in San Antonio, croissants in New Orleans or iced chocolate muffins on the Plaza in Santa Fe, where, fortunately, we ate outdoors on a park bench.

Not once did we eat breakfast in a traditional restaurant or fast-food place. The closest we came was at the KOA Kampground just outside Glacier National Park, where we ate "Montana-sized" pancakes that were the size of our paper plates. They were good, but at $3.75 apiece for blueberry pancakes, they also added up to a Montana-sized bill for breakfast.

Our best breakfasts came at the Western Pleasure Guest Ranch near Sandpoint, Idaho: egg casserole, sausage, pancakes, cereal, homemade cherry pastry, juice and coffee. One of the best parts of breakfast was being able to finish our meal in leisure and enjoy a second cup of coffee, while watching through the lodge's tall windows as the resident border collie taught our children how to play fetch.

Lunches were daily highlights, not because of the food but the settings. We picnicked in parks and playgrounds all over the country, often finding them after talking with greeters at local visitors' centers or checkout clerks at grocery stores.

We laid out our blanket and enjoyed peanut butter-and-jelly sandwiches on a riverbank in Yellowstone National Park, on lake shores with backdrops of snow-capped peaks in Grand Teton National Park in Wyoming and Waterton Lakes National Park in Canada, and beneath a towering canopy of giant redwoods in Humboldt Redwoods State Park in northern California. At meals in places such as those, we needed our cameras as much as our napkins.

The scenery changed from picnic to picnic, but the fare usually didn't.

Peanut butter. Ah, peanut butter. We consumed more than six pounds of the stuff — crunchy and creamy — over seven weeks.

But when we stopped at grocery stores, we also occasionally bought sliced turkey and ham and even fried chicken — foods that were sure to last us a few meals.

We started our trip eating this way partly for economical reasons and partly because we traveled through some pretty rural areas, where towns and meal times didn't always coincide. In places like Iowa and South Dakota, it was a lot easier to find a park or a roadside picnic table than a restaurant with something everyone will eat.

But we enjoyed numerous meals in restaurants along the way. Some of the more notable ones:

* In Dyersville, Iowa, we stumbled onto the Country Junction, where we ate baked ham and

Ah, peanut butter. We consumed more than six pounds of the stuff — crunchy and creamy — over seven weeks.

fried chicken, catfish, shrimp and drank at least a gallon of iced tea.

* In Glacier National Park at the Rising Sun Motel restaurant, we enjoyed grilled trout and squash, vegetarian pasta, spaghetti marinara, and a grilled cheese sandwich.

* In Brookings, Ore., a small town on the Pacific coast near the California border, we wandered down to the harbor for a late lunch at The Hungry Clam, a small place with big plates of seafood: shrimp, calamari, cod and clams. I had a bread bowl — a round loaf of sourdough with the middle carved out — of homemade clam chowder that was outstanding. It kept me going for two days.

* In San Francisco, good eating was easy.

We ate thick hamburgers and chicken sandwiches — washed down with wonderful and, at that point in the trip, much-needed samples of freshly brewed beer — at the San Francisco Brewing Co., which was launched by University of Virginia alumnus Allan G. Paul 15 years ago as the city's first brewpub. Paul also gave us a tour of his operation, which is housed in an historic tavern on the edge of the city's North Beach and Chinatown sections.

We wandered through Chinatown and had a fine meal of soup and fried rice at a small, upstairs restaurant — Hong Kong Clay Pot — on Grant Avenue, one of Chinatown's main thoroughfares.

We topped off our San Francisco visit with dinner at Alioto's, a venerable seafood restaurant on Fisherman's Wharf. The five of us ate salmon, shrimp and a variety of pasta. It was a fancy meal by our standards, with first-rate service, and a view of the Golden Gate Bridge as the sun dipped behind it.

* In Winslow, Ariz., Phat Mico's was a nice little discovery, a small place near the edge of town, suggested by fellow guests at the hotel where we were staying. It served gourmet food at reasonable prices.

* In San Antonio, we did what lots of other tourists — and locals — do and that's eat at Mi Tierra Cafe & Bakery, a large, well-established Tex-Mex restaurant at Market Square. It features good food, professional service and wandering musicians.

For breakfast, I walked a few blocks each morning from our hotel near Alamo Plaza to Beignets Coffeehouse on the River Walk and fetched hot beignets for everyone and coffee for me (other members of my family get their caffeine elsewhere).

* In New Orleans, we dined at two fine places in the French Quarter, getting our fill of jambalaya

It was a fancy meal by our standards, with first-rate service, and a view of the Golden Gate Bridge as the sun dipped behind it.

An Original *WebPointers*™ Interactive Internet Guide

and po-boys and other good stuff, but the most memorable meal we ate in the city of great food was at Lama's, an unpretentious seafood market and restaurant, just east of New Orleans off I-10. It was recommended by the fellow who led us on a swamp tour just up the road. "You know it's good," he said, "because the locals eat there." He and the locals are right. The boiled shrimp and soft-shelled crab were superb. And inexpensive.

* In Pensacola Beach, Peg Leg Pete's Oyster Bar was our place. It came recommended by a local and we ate dinner there three nights. The fresh seafood was quite good and, as an added bonus, the kids' meals came in green sand buckets (without the sand), in which they carried their leftovers back to the motel. There was a playground, cold beer, a genial wait staff, and, considering the competition we checked, reasonable prices. That's a grand slam for parents traveling with kids.

We did most of our camping on the northern leg of our trip, which means that's when we did most of our cooking. We had purchased a two-burner, propane camp stove before leaving home. We didn't cook anything that would rate an appearance on The Food Channel, but we prepared filling stuff: pasta, rice, baked beans. The kids enjoyed the stove, mostly I think, because we boiled water for hot chocolate on cold mornings.

Other than that, we ate ballpark food and buffalo burgers and our share of fast-food: hamburgers, hot dogs, roast beef sandwiches and tacos. Sometimes, Hardee's, Wendy's, Subway and fast-food taco places in the Southwest (where you see local features such as salsa bars) were just too hard — and convenient — to pass up.

Funny thing, after all of the miles and meals, one of our favorite dinners was one we prepared ourselves. It was at the Idaho ranch, where our cabin had a kitchen — the only kitchen we saw during our seven weeks on the road. We cooked rice and broccoli and soup. Pretty basic stuff that doesn't sound like much. But it sure tasted like home.

KOA Kampground (http://www.koa.com/where/mt/26121.htm)
Rising Sun Motor Inn — Two Dogs Flats Grill (http://www.glacierparkinc.com/DINE.htm)
Western Pleasure Guest Ranch (http://www.westernpleasureranch.com)
San Francisco Brewing Co. (http://www.sfbrewing.com)
Alioto's (http://www.fishermanswharf.org/Alioto.htm)
Mi Tierra Cafe & Bakery (http://sanantonio.citysearch.com/E/V/SATTX/0001/54/53)

Funny thing, after all of the miles and meals, one of our favorite dinners was one we prepared ourselves.

Animals appeared everywhere we went

My mother was stunned.

She couldn't believe I allowed a camel to kiss me in Washington.

Or that I rode a horse in Idaho, hopped out of the van to shoot photographs of a bear in California, and held an alligator in Louisiana.

My mother knows me well, and she knows I'm not an animal-lover, so she was intrigued to read in The Times-Dispatch, along with everyone else, of my exploits involving animals on our cross-country trip.

Rodents, reptiles, it doesn't much matter. I don't even like dogs very much.

I am an admirer of animals and an admirer of people who love animals, but I'm not particularly fond of them. My philosophy is, just because I enjoy seeing an animal in a zoo or wildlife refuge doesn't mean I want one peeing on my living room rug.

But much of our trip, much to my surprise, involved animals in some way. I suppose it's because animals are such a part of the American landscape and the country's history.

We saw snakes and alligators and elk and bison and possums and skunks and a single black bear. As we traveled through the northern Rockies, we were constantly on the lookout for grizzlies, although we saw none.

We visited two aquariums, one zoo, a Sea World, and a ranch where exotic animals roam.

Everywhere we went, we were looking for animals or cleaning up crumbs in our van or campsite so they wouldn't come looking for us.

We had some interesting moments.

At a campground at Gulf Islands National Seashore on the Florida panhandle, Melissa came nose-to-nose with a skunk — she was inside the tent, and it was outside, on the other side of the screen — in the middle of the night. She didn't scream. We were grateful.

Despite the thousands of miles we drove and hiked through prime bear country, we saw only one — a small, black bear in Prairie Creek Redwoods State Park in northern California. He seemed to be mugging for those motorists, us included, who stopped along the roadside, got out of our vehicles and used up all of our film as he loped along to nowhere in particular. I'm not convinced it wasn't a guy in a bear suit.

... much of our trip, much to my surprise, involved animals in some way. I suppose it's because animals are such a part of the American land-scape and the country's history.

An Original *WebPointers*™ Interactive Internet Guide

In Custer State Park in South Dakota where buffalo roam freely, we arrived just before sunset and paid the $10 entrance fee but figured we were too late to see any bison. We were wrong. Not far into the park, we hit the brakes and came to a stop in a traffic jam. The reason: a herd of bison was casually walking on the road toward us. They passed by on either side of Big Blue. We could have rolled down our windows and touched them. But we didn't. Everywhere we went, we read and heard warnings about how dangerous bison can be. Still, we got a fabulous view. It was the best $10 we spent all trip.

However, our most memorable animal encounter — and our most memorable bison — came in Yellowstone National Park.

For lunch one day, we picnicked next to the Yellowstone River, near Le Hardy Rapids in the central part of the park. Before taking a little hike along the river, we returned to the van to stash our leftovers. On the road, nearby, was a bison.

Traffic stopped in both directions while the bison meandered along the two-lane highway. Not being able to go anywhere, we stood and watched.

Rangers recommend you get no closer than 25 yards to bison. They look like big hairy cows, but they are very fast and can be very rough, and, according to official National Park Service literature, they injure humans more often than bears.

We kept our distance, but the bison moved behind our parked van and appeared to be making his way down the road. We decided to continue our hike and returned to the riverbank. A while later, on our way back to the van, we noticed a rather large object between us and Big Blue: the bison. It had wandered off the road and found a shady spot in our path.

To recap:

We're on a narrow trail. We've got the river on one side, and an extremely large bison on the other. I had a flashback to the time I was working a summer job at Paramount's Kings Dominion years ago and an ostrich chased me into a pond. That's another story.

I was also thinking about — and regretting — that buffalo burger I'd eaten two states back.

Eyes wide and hearts pumping, we quietly walked farther down the riverside trail, well out of our way but also out of the bison's. I sent Robin and the kids toward the far end of the parking area and, while the bison wasn't looking, I sneaked to the van. I fired up Big Blue and quickly backed to

... our most memorable animal encounter — and our most memorable bison — came in Yellowstone National Park.

where they were waiting, a safe distance from the bison. I stepped on the gas and we headed toward Montana.

I believe the bison couldn't have cared less that we were anywhere near. I think it just wanted a little peace and quiet and a respite from noisy tourists driving by and snapping photos. But it makes for a good story.

Back in the van Jack burst into song to celebrate my moment of heroic glory. To the tune of "Grandma Got Run Over by a Reindeer," he sang: "Daddy got run over by a buffalo!"

Not quite, but it's nice to be loved.

Custer State Park (http://www.state.sd.us/sdparks/custer/resorts.htm)
Prairie Creek Redwoods State Park (http://www.cal-parks.ca.gov/north/ncrd/pcrsp.htm)

Back in the van Jack burst into song to celebrate my moment of heroic glory.

Looking back

I could tell you our trip was flawless in its planning and execution, that our accommodations, meals and moods were always ideal, that the five of us cheerfully hurtled down the highway each day, holding hands and singing "Kum Ba Ya."

I could tell you that, but I'd be lying.

Fact is, we weren't "The Brady Bunch" on wheels. We had a singular opportunity and a wonderful time and things went remarkably well, but we also had what I will charitably call "moments."

After all, we were a family on the road, not a figment of some television producer's fertile imagination.

Over the course of seven weeks, we heard plenty of complaints and whining. Every day, it seemed, someone threw a tantrum. More than once, Melissa muttered, "You've ruined my summer vacation!" I must also say, however, that within hours, at the next stop down the road, her sentiment usually changed to, "This is the best place I've ever been!"

Alexandra, the bounciest of our children, had her own way of expressing displeasure, whether it was howling, exchanging slaps with her sister, or being generally uncooperative.

Jack's favorite method of protest was to decline, momentarily, to be buckled into his safety seat. He also has developed particular tastes at his tender age and one of his great dislikes turned out to be those portable toilets you find in the wilderness and other out-of-the-way places. Whenever he had to use one, he demanded one of us hold his nose while he conducted his business.

And we'll never forget his fit in Death Valley, during which he kicked and screamed for what seemed like 10 hours — it was more like 10 minutes — in the parking lot of a museum in 120-degree heat. The reason for his outburst: we don't know. I believe we can attribute it to his being 3.

Despite all of that, things did not go nearly as badly as I had feared they might. We spent six months excitedly making arrangements — determining our itinerary, investigating lodging, and making contact with people we hoped to meet along the way. We also spent six months worrying about how the kids would react to seven weeks of traveling in a van.

Our apprehension proved to be largely unfounded. As it turned out, they did pretty well. In fact, the riding itself was not much of a problem, even on the days of our longest drives; we had four

... we also had what I will charitably call "moments." After all, we were a family on the road, not a figment of some television producer's fertile imagination.

days when we covered more than 500 miles and numerous days when we drove more than 300. I thought for sure somewhere along the way the kids would lock arms and chain themselves to a motel room door and absolutely refuse to get back into the van.

We had no locked arms, no human chains.

Just those "moments." As my mother-in-law correctly reminded us after our return, families have "moments" every day at home. We simply experienced every tantrum, irritation and bad mood more acutely because we were living and traveling in very close quarters. Sometimes we dealt with these situations well, sometimes not. But the sun always came up the next day and we went on.

In planning the trip, we obviously took the kids into consideration. When we could, we gave them a choice. But we didn't turn every stop into a referendum. Robin and I made most of the decisions ourselves, but we made those decisions with the kids in mind.

Some of our destinations were distinctly kid-friendly, but mostly we were seeking places that were interesting. We wanted our children to enjoy themselves, but we also wanted them to learn something.

We often stopped for lunch or breaks at parks or playgrounds. Sometimes I felt we were on a playground tour of America. But they served us well, allowing the kids to get their wiggles out and us to catch our breath. Or, at least, take a deep one.

We truly didn't catch our breath until we reached the Gulf Coast near the end of our journey. We went hard day after day for the seven weeks we were on the road and for weeks leading up to our trip. That's one of the things I'd do differently if we were to plan another extensive trip. I would clear the calendar for a week or two before leaving.

For this trip, Robin and I both worked at our jobs — she as a systems analyst for a bank — up to the last minute, plus I had a medical issue arise that proved to be minor but was worrisome at the time and required doctors' visits and tests the week before our departure. Forget about wondering what to pack, we were wondering if we were even going; the trip itself was in jeopardy only a few days before we were to leave. That's no way to enter a seven-week expedition, but it's exactly how we did it.

We did pretty well preparing an itinerary; we did less well preparing ourselves.

Disorganization, in general, plagued us. We spent too much time fumbling around the van, looking for things we needed and couldn't find. We would pack lighter for any future trip: fewer

Sometimes I felt we were on a playground tour of America. But they served us well, allowing the kids to get their wiggles out and us to catch our breath.

An Original WebPointers™ Interactive Internet Guide

clothes and fewer toys. We would visit coin laundries more often or simply smell worse. Who would care? And the kids could entertain themselves with items we pick up along the way.

So, those are some of the things we regret. There were many more things we did not regret or that we were flat-out grateful for.

We experienced no serious illnesses. Each of the kids had an incident or two of motion sickness, although we think Jack threw up as we waited to pull into a parking garage in Santa Fe because he gagged himself with a baby wipe he was using to tidy up. Otherwise, no one broke any bones or got bit by anything, other than an occasional mosquito or, in Alex's case, Jack.

We were blessed with good weather and good fortune on the road. We had no wrecks and received no speeding tickets. I had a fight with an unusually high curb in Kentucky and roughed up the running board on the passenger side of Big Blue, but it was nothing serious. We had a dead battery in St. Louis — I left the interior lights on overnight — but a quick jump got us rolling again.

Otherwise, we negotiated mountain passes in the Rockies, tore across the desert Southwest, and gingerly picked our way through urban mazes such as St. Louis, San Francisco and Atlanta without incident. We even survived a lengthy detour on a dirt road in Wyoming.

We got lost a minimum number of times and all of them, strangely enough, were my fault. Who needs a map? For instance, we arrived in San Antonio well after dark and wound up in a section of town most tourists — and San Antonio residents, for that matter — don't see. All because I didn't bother consulting a map.

Robin was driving, I was navigating — and I use the term loosely. I relied on instinct. Of course, I'd never set foot in San Antonio. Neither had my instinct. We missed our exit on the interstate. As I riffled through papers looking for a map, I suggested another exit. That just made matters worse, putting us on another limited-access road that carried us farther away from where we needed to be and into what surely looked like harm's way. We switched places. I drove, Robin located a map and we found our hotel in a matter of minutes.

We did not lose our way often, but we did lose a few things, including a wide-angle camera lens in the Midwest and a tube of toothpaste in the Florida Panhandle. Alex lost a tooth in Yellowstone and her favorite swimming goggles in Las Vegas. My eyeglasses broke along the way, but I fortunately had packed a backup pair.

However, we did not lose any kids — although Alex became temporarily misplaced in a shop in San Francisco's Chinatown. A woman working at the store approached Robin and asked if she had

... no one broke any bones or got bit by anything, other than an occasional mosquito or, in Alex's case, Jack.

a little girl. She led Robin to the front of the store where a teary Alex was being comforted by a host of nice Chinese women.

We traveled almost 10,000 miles in 51 days. We dropped in on 28 states, as well as Canada and Mexico. We dangled our toes in the chilly northern Pacific; we body-surfed in the warm waters of the Gulf of Mexico. We waded in rivers and streams everywhere.

We visited ballparks and theme parks and national parks. We rode horses in Idaho, cable cars in San Francisco and a tram to the top of the Gateway Arch in St. Louis. We shivered in Oregon, sweated in Florida and felt like we were darn near dying in Death Valley. We were stopped — and released — by a border patrol in Texas.

We crossed the Mississippi River twice and the Continental Divide a half-dozen times. We saw historic missions and glittery casinos, and sometimes they were just across the parking lot from each other.

We spent 16 days on Central Daylight time, 14 on Pacific Daylight, 13 on Mountain Daylight, six on Eastern Daylight and two on Mountain Standard (parts of Arizona do not recognize daylight-savings time).

It was a summer ... we will never forget. And we will never look at a map of the United States in the same way again.

Time and again we proved the adage that traveling is about the journey, not simply the destination. We had great luck with brief stops along the way, such as Abraham Lincoln's boyhood farm in southern Indiana and the Tuskegee Institute National Historic Site in Alabama. At the latter, the kids learned more about George Washington Carver, a quiet giant in American history and — most importantly — inventor of peanut butter.

We visited obvious landmarks such as Mount Rushmore but also stumbled onto some unscheduled delights, such as Sunset Crater National Monument, in northern Arizona, where, just before sunset one evening, we visited pitch-black lava fields that haven't changed much in more than 800 years.

It was a summer — including the burning daily issue of creamy versus crunchy peanut butter — we will never forget. And we will never look at a map of the United States in the same way again.

We always believed our journey to see America would be a great education. While we were on the road, it was hard to tell what, besides a lot of T-shirts and souvenirs, the kids would bring home with them. It turns out, a lot.

It has been most gratifying to watch Jack work a U.S. map puzzle and have something to say about each state as he puts it in place, or to listen as Alex discusses something she learned at the Alamo, or to know that Melissa can carry on a conversation about something she saw in Texas or California.

Because I chronicled our trip in The Times-Dispatch, I heard from many readers who said our experiences reminded them of their own family vacations. Others said our trip has motivated them to consider taking one of their own.

We had never taken a trip remotely resembling this one. Robin and I had traveled to California for 10 days before we had children and to Colorado another time when we had only one child.

In one sense, this trip was a distinct challenge with three children and a busy daily schedule, but in another it was truly liberating. On the road and far away from home, we were freed from the day-to-day constraints of real life, which enabled us to adopt an entirely different mindset. At home for example, we would think twice about making a trip to the grocery store in the evening for fear of disrupting our routine; on the road, we thought nothing of driving 200 miles after dinner. We wrung as much from every day — and from ourselves — as we could.

My advice if you think you'd like to take a trip like ours: do it. But be sure you know what you're getting into.

For instance, seven weeks sounds like an eternity — and there were days when it felt like it — but it really isn't if you're planning to cover as much ground as we did. We did an awful lot everywhere we went, but there were so many things we missed because of time constraints. We averaged almost 200 miles a day, which is not unreasonable, but if you stay a few days at any one spot, that creates some long rides down the road.

We headed out in the heart of prime tourist season — July and August — in most of these places. Unless you're willing to remove your school-age kids from class for an extended period, summer is the only time you can schedule a lengthy trip.

If you can avoid the middle of summer, however, late spring or early fall would probably be better times to travel. Crowds would certainly be thinner, and it surely would be cooler in St. Louis, San Antonio and Death Valley.

But you have to be careful about the winter weather in some places; Glacier, Yellowstone and Yosemite national parks come immediately to mind. Significant snows can fall in the higher elevations as early as October and some mountain passes, such as Glacier's Going-to-the-Sun Road, do not begin to be cleared until May.

My advice if you think you'd like to take a trip like ours: do it.

We made a number of good purchases but none was smarter than the National Parks pass. It cost $50, saved us a considerable sum and is good for a year.

High-rise hotels are wonderful — we enjoyed some very comfortable nights staying in big-time hotels in St. Louis and San Francisco — but, frankly, some of the lower-priced, park-at-your-door motels were far more convenient for us. It's a lot easier to carry in armloads of luggage and sleeping children when you don't have to trudge through parking garages and ride elevators.

We made a number of good purchases but none was smarter than the National Parks pass. It cost $50, saved us a considerable sum and is good for a year.

Inevitably after such an adventure, people want to know what you liked best.

My cop-out answer is, "Everything."

But it's true. I enjoyed every place we went. Naturally, I was smitten with hanging out behind the batting cage at Busch Stadium in St. Louis, watching Mark McGwire drive pitch after pitch into the leftfield bleachers. And I got chills playing catch with my kids on the "Field of Dreams" in Iowa. And it was a kick to be standing on a corner in Winslow, Arizona.

The national parks were beyond words and the cities brought us back to civilization. And so many places — the Western Pleasure Guest Ranch in Sandpoint, Idaho, stands out among many — showed us just how nice people can be.

Still, we all had our favorite stops.

Robin most enjoyed Yellowstone and Glacier.

Melissa most liked our day at Sea World in San Antonio, which happened to fall on her 13th birthday. She also enjoyed gift shops everywhere.

Alex said her favorite places were the Grand Canyon and the "kitty barn." At the guest ranch in Sandpoint, a mother cat and her kittens had taken up residence in a corner of a horse barn. Our kids spent considerable time just chasing and hugging and playing with the kitties.

Jack loves tractors and still talks about his visit to Iowa, where we stopped in the National Farm Toy Museum and then went across the street to an Ertl outlet store. Ertl is one of the world's leading manufacturers of farm toys. Second place on his list: the Idaho kitty barn. Third: the hot, spring-fed pool at Death Valley.

Are we closer as a family, as a result of the trip? I'm not sure I'd say that, although there were times on the trip I felt we had become some sort of five-headed monster. In the long run, I imagine, we will find it helped us learn to live together more harmoniously. Or not.

Close quarters breed familiarity and contempt — and funny moments. It was interesting to watch the kids align against one another — or against us — or buddy up in pairs. Alex and Jack, being closer in age, do that most often. The results are not always appropriate, but usually instructive.

In a restaurant in Atlanta, Robin took the two of them to the bathroom before dinner. Alex and Jack entered the same stall to take care of things. From behind the closed door, Robin heard giggling. "Now," said Jack, "we can use bathroom words."

Would we do it again? Well, we had been back only a few days when we began reminiscing. So, the answer is yes.

But it was tiring.

We rode hard. I think we grew numb to the miles and miles and just accepted the driving that faced us most days. There were so many things we didn't get a chance to do, but when we look back on this trip I'm sure we will be amazed at all we did: hiking, swimming, picnicking, sightseeing and simply trying to immerse ourselves, however short the time, in the place we were visiting.

We were so busy that although the kids watched an occasional video while riding in the van, not once in seven weeks did they turn on a motel television.

Working during all of this added an interesting dimension for me. It made me juggle the hours. I wrote while Robin drove, but I had to do much of my work after the kids went to bed.

Still, the technology involved was incredible. We couldn't have taken this trip and chronicled it — at least not in this manner — a few years ago. I used a laptop computer to transmit my stories as well as photographs from a digital camera. I kept in touch with a digital cellular phone, by e-mail and through the Web site The Times-Dispatch built for the trip. All of this led me to crave electricity, which made camping for days at a time difficult.

Memorable scene: Alex standing guard outside a women's bathroom in a Yellowstone campground, the laptop re-charging inside, and hollering to us each time someone went inside to use the facilities. We had to yank her off sentry duty. We were looking for a little more subtle warning system if someone were to walk off with the laptop. She misunderstood her role and thought she was supposed to be a public address announcer.

We spent so long planning our trip and thinking about it and wondering how it would go, that it's hard to believe it's come and gone. It went fast.

I'm sure as the years go by we'll forget the rough patches of the trip. I'm just hoping the kids

Close quarters breed familiarity and contempt — and funny moments. It was interesting to watch them align against one another — or against us — or buddy up in pairs.

remember all of the good times. Considering the 80 rolls of film we shot, the 1,000 digital-camera frames stored on our computer and the bags and boxes of souvenirs, books and brochures we came home with and will require years to organize, I don't imagine there's any way they can forget.

One reader, who followed our adventures through the newspaper stories, told me early on in our journey, "It will always be referred to in your family as 'The Trip.'"

I hope so.

Tuskegee Institute Historic Site: (http://www.nps.gov/tuin)
Sunset Crater National Monument (http://www.nps.gov/sucr/)

One reader, who followed our adventures through the newspaper stories, told me early on in our journey, "It will always be referred to in your family as 'The Trip.'

Website Appendix

AAA (http://www.aaamidatlantic.com)

Abraham Lincoln's Boyhood Farm (http://www.nps.gov/libo)

Alcatraz (http://www.nps.gov/alcatraz/welcome.html)

Alioto's (http://www.fishermanswharf.org/Alioto.htm)

Anasazi Heritage Center (http://www.swcolo.org/Tourism/Archaeology/AnasaziHeritageCenter.html)

Atlanta Braves (http://www.atlantabraves.com)

Badlands National Park (http://www.nps.gov/badl/)

Badwater (http://www.coolspots.com/spots/iny/page203001.html)

Bally's (http://www.ballyslv.com/)

Balmorehea State Park (http://www.geocities.com/pipeline/ramp/8975/html/texdivesites.html)

Bayou Sauvage National Wildlife Refuge (http://southeastlouisiana.fws.gov/bsed.html)

Bellagio Resort (http://las.vegas.hotelguide.net/data/h100011.htm)

Big Chicken (http://www.bigchicken.com/history.html)

Blackfeet Indian Reservation (http://www.blackfeetnation.com)

Bridge of the Gods (http://www.teleport.com/%7Esisemo/legends/bridge_gods.htm)

Buffalo Bill Historical Center (http://www.bbhc.org)

Buffalo Bill Museum (http://www.bbhc.org/bbm_firstpage.html)

Cody Firearms Museum (http://www.bbhc.org/cfm_firstpage.html)

Cody Rodeo (http://www.codystampederodeo.org/)

Columbia River Gorge (http://www.fs.fed.us/r6/columbia)

Corn Palace (http://www.cornpalace.org/cornpalace.html)

Dallesport (http://klickitatcounty.org/Tourism/about)

Dante's View (http://geology.wr.usgs.gov/docs/usgsnps/deva/ftdan1.html)

Daughters of the Republic of Texas (http://www.drtl.org/drt_info.html)

Death Valley National Park (http://www.nps.gov/deva)

Devils Tower National Monument (http://www.nps.gov/deto/home.htm)

Don Henley (http://www.donhenley.com)

Douthat State Park (http://www.dcr.state.va.us/parks/douthat.htm)

El Paso Convention & Visitors Bureau (http://www.elpasocvb.com)

El Paso, TX (http://www.ci.el-paso.tx.us)

Ertl Toy Outlet (http://www.ertltoys.com)

Exploratorium (http://www.exploratorium.edu)

Field of Dreams (http://www.fieldofdreamsmoviesite.com/distance.html)

Fisherman's Wharf (http://www.fishermanswharf.org/)

Ford African Rain Forest (http://www.zooatlanta.org/anim_exh_farf.html)

Fort Pickens (http://www.tulane.edu/~latner/Pickens.html)

Furnace Creek Inn & Ranch Resort (http://www.furnacecreekresort.com/frame-pn.htm)

Ghiradelli Square (http://www.ghirardellisq.com)

Glacier Park Boat Co. (http://www.digisys.net/gpboats/welcome.htm)

Going-to-the-Sun Road (http://glacier.visitmt.com/sunpr.htm)

Grand Canyon National Park (http://www.nps.gov/grca)

Grand Teton National Park (http://www.grand.teton.national-park.com)

Gulf Islands National Seashore (http://www.nps.gov/guis)

Hampton Inn Pensacola Beach (http://www.hampton-inn.com)

Hannibal, MO (http://hanmo.com/jcs/)

Happy Isles Nature Center (http://geology.csun.edu/yosemite/hi.html)

Historic Pensacola Village (http://www.dos.state.fl.us/dhr/pensacola)

Hoover Dam (http://www.hooverdam.com)

Hotel Inter-Continental (http://www.neworleanshotel.com/promotions.html)

Humboldt Redwoods State Park (http://parks.ca.gov/north/ncrd/hrsp.html)

Idaho Travel and Tourism (http://www.visitid.org)

Institute of Texan Cultures (http://www.texancultures.utsa.edu/main)

International Museum of the Horse (http://www.imh.org/)

Jefferson National Expansion Memorial (http://www.nps.gov/jeff/Default.htm)

John Pugh, Master of Tromp L'oeil Murals (http://www.illusion-art.com)

Kentucky Horse Park (http://www.kyhorsepark.com/khp/hp1.html)

Kit Carson Home and Museum (http://taosvacationguide.com/MAT/kit.html)

KOA Kampground (http://www.koa.com/where/mt/26121.htm)

L&M's Eagles Fastlane (http://www.eaglesfans.com)

La Fonda Hotel (http://www.santafe.org/lafonda/index.html)

La Posada (http://www.laposada.org/)

Lama's Seafood Restaurant and Market (http://www.fishing-boating.com/lamas/)

Las Vegas Convention & Visitors Authority (http://www.lasvegas24hours.com)
Left and Center Field of Dreams (http://www.leftandcenterfod.com/)
Loretto Chapel (http://www.lorettochapel.com/html/stair.html)
Man o' War (http://www.imh.org/imh/kyhpl6b.html#xtocid1228611)
Marriott Pavilion Hotel (http://www.marriotthotels.com/stlpv/)
Martinez Hacienda (http://www.laplaza.org/art/museums_mtz.php3)
Maswik Lodge (http://www.grand-canyon.az.us/serv/gc_pl_ml.htm)
Mary Garner-Mitchell Illustration & Design (http://www.garnermitchell.com)
Maymont Foundation ((http://www.maymont.org)
Menger Hotel (http://www.historicmenger.com)
Mesa Verde National Park (http://www.nps.gov/meve/)
MGM Grand Hotel (http://www.mgmgrand.com/lv/pages/index_home.shtml)
Mi Tierra Cafe & Bakery (http://sanantonio.citysearch.com/E/V/SATTX/0001/54/53)
Mission San Jose (http://www.nps.gov/saan/saanjo01.htm)
Mission Ysleta (http://elpasoparishes.org/MisHisYsleta.htm)
Mount Rushmore National Memorial (http://www.nps.gov/moru)
Mount Whitney (http://www.nps.gov/seki/whitney.htm)
Museum of Westward Expansion (http://www.gatewayarch.com/museum.html)
National Farm Toy Museum (http://www.dyersville.org/museum.htm)
National Museum of Naval Aviation (http://www.naval-air.org)
Nebraska Division of Tourism & Travel (http://www.visitnebraska.org)
New Orleans Convention & Visitors Bureau (http://www.neworleanscvb.com)
New Orleans Swamp Tours (http://southeastlouisiana.fws.gov/bsed.html)
Oregon Coast Aquarium (http://www.aquarium.org)
Oregon Tourism Commission (http://www.traveloregon.com)
Palace of Fine Arts (http://www.exploratorium.edu/palace/index.html)
Palmer Family (http://www.proaxis.com/~joes/palmer/index.htm)
Paramount's Kings Dominion ((http://www.kingsdominion.com)
Peg Leg Pete's Oyster Bar (http://www.peglegpetes.com/restaurant.html)
Petrified Forest National Park (http://www.nps.gov/pefo/)
Pier 39 (http://www.pier39.com)
Plains Indian Museum (http://www.bbhc.org/pim_reinstallation.html)

Prairie Creek Redwoods State Park (http://www.cal-parks.ca.gov/north/ncrd/pcrsp.htm)

Prince of Wales Hotel (http://www.fortsaskinfo.com/photos13.htm)

Rand McNally TripMaker and StreetFinder (http://www.randmcnally.com)

Recreational Vehicle Industry Association (http://www.rvia.org)

Richmond Times-Dispatch (http://www.timesdispatch.com)

Rising Sun Motor Inn — Two Dogs Flats Grill (http://www.glacierparkinc.com/DINE.htm)

River Walk (http://www.stic.net/users/sarwt)

San Antonio Convention & Visitors Bureau (http://www.sanantoniocvb.com)

San Fernando Cathedral (http://www.sfcathedral.org)

San Francisco Brewing Co. (http://www.sfbrewing.com)

Santa Fe Convention and Visitors Bureau (http://www.santafe.org)

Schreiner Farms (http://www.idahomall.com/elkcompany)

Sea World (http://www.seaworld.com)

South Dakota Department of Tourism (http://www.travelsd.com)

St. Louis Cardinals (http://www.stlcardinals.com/)

St. Louis Convention & Visitors Commission (http://www.explorestlouis.com)

Standin' on the Corner Park (http://www.winslowarizona.com/)

Sunset Crater National Monument (http://www.nps.gov/sucr/)

Take it Easy (http://www.illusion-art.com/winslow/music.html)

The Alamo (http://www.thealamo.org)

The Dalles (http://www.el.com/To/TheDalles)

The Peachoid (http://www.roadsideamerica.com/attract/SCGAFpeach.html)

Tower of the Americas (http://www.toweroftheamericas.com)

Tuolumne Meadows (http://www.sierragatewaymap.com/tmr.html)

Tuskegee Institute Historic Site: (http://www.nps.gov/tuin)

Underground Atlanta (http://www.underatl.com)

University of Kentucky Wildcats (http://www.ukathletics.com)

Vanworks (http://www.vanworks.com)

Wall Drug (http://www.walldrug.com)

Wall, SD (http://www.wall-badlands.com/)

Waterton-Glacier International Peace Park (http://www.americanparknetwork.com/parkinfo/gl/index.html)

Wayne Chicken Show (http://www.chickenshow.com/)

Western Pleasure Guest Ranch (http://www.westernpleasureranch.com)
Whitney Gallery of Western Art (http://www.bbhc.org/wgwa_firstpage.html)
World of Coca-Cola (http://www.roadsideamerica.com/attract/GAATLcoke.html)
Yellowstone National Park (http://www.nps.gov/yell/home.htm)
Yosemite Concession Services Corp (http://www.yosemitepark.com)
Yosemite Lodge (http://www.nps.gov/yose/planning/gmp/lodge.html)
Yosemite National Park (http://www.nps.gov/yose/home.htm)
Zoo Atlanta (http://www.zooatlanta.org/splash3.html)

Acknowledgments

When embarking on an adventure such as this — a cross-country trip and, ultimately, a book — you need all the help you can get.

We were fortunate to get a lot.

Dozens and dozens of people helped make the trip a success and the book a reality. When I say we couldn't have done it without them, I'm not kidding. We never would have escaped our driveway if left to our own devices. Some who provided assistance were old friends, others were new ones we met along the way. Some of their names show up elsewhere in this book; others do not, although their help was most appreciated, whether they provided us information in their roles at convention and visitors bureaus, gave us smiles and directions at state welcome centers, or simply allowed us to use their phone.

The problem here is I cannot name everyone who lent a helping hand. I wish I could list every single person, but I'm aware it's bad form for the acknowledgment section to be longer than the rest of the book. So, I offer a blanket "Thank you" and a sincere apology for the inadequate recognition.

But there are a few people I feel compelled to thank publicly: My editors at the Richmond Times-Dispatch — Bill Millsaps, Louise Seals, Howard Owen and Bob Walsh — who were supportive from the moment I proposed this harebrained scheme.

My colleagues at the paper, particularly Mary Garner-Mitchell, who designed the series logo (which serves as the cover of this book) and who was the first to blurt out "Are we there yet!?" during an early brainstorming meeting; photographer Masaaki Okada who exhibited grace, patience and good humor in shooting the cover photo; Jim Caiella and George Lamm for their photographic advice; Hadi YazdanPanah for his technical guidance; my editors in the Flair department, particularly Karin Kapsidelis, for handling the original series; Blanche Wilder and Kymberly Haas for tirelessly keeping our Web site updated while we were on the road; and Times-Dispatch promotions director Amy Chown for her willingness to promote the daylights out of the series.

The Dallas and Graham families, whose travels inspired our journey.

The Recreational Vehicle Industry Association and Jon Tancredi of Barton Gilanelli and Associates, who helped us secure a conversion van for the trip, and Keith Hess of Vanworks Inc., Fort Collins, Colo., from whose company we leased "Big Blue," which became part of the family.

Special thanks to ...

My friend and newspaper colleague Tom Mullen, who was most generous with his counsel, kindness and editing skills, which were, as always, invaluable and most welcome.

My mother Betty Lohmann, who took in our mail, watered the azaleas and kept the home fires burning while we were gone.

My mother-in-law Mary Little, who kept the e-mails coming as we traveled around the country.

My siblings — brother Steve and sisters Anne and Charlotte — and their families for their support and encouragement.

My children — Melissa, Alexandra and Jack — who always provide good material and teach me something new every day. And not once during our trip, did they wrestle me to the ground when I said, "Creamy or crunchy?" or "OK, let's get in the van!"

And to my wife Robin, who is my friend, partner, cheerleader and personal copy editor.

Thank you all.

About Bill Lohmann

Bill Lohmann is an award-winning feature writer and columnist for the Richmond Times-Dispatch. He previously worked for the Charlottesville Daily Progress, The Richmond News Leader and United Press International bureaus in Richmond, Orlando and Atlanta. He is a native Richmonder and a graduate of the University of Richmond. This is his first book.

The design for *Are We There Yet? A Modern American Family's Cross-Country Adventure*, reflects the influence of Master Typographer Jan Tschichold. The horizontal proportions were chosen to offer the best onscreen presentation for the companion eBook edition which is published in Adobe System's Portable Document Format. Text is typeset in Gill Sans, headlines in Giovanni Book. Printing and binding by LithoColor Press of Westchester, IL.

Recommend this Book to a Friend

If you have found *Are We There Yet?* to be a useful and valuable resource please recommend it to your friends. The printed edition is available from fine booksellers everywhere and may also be ordered online. Those who want to know more about it immediately, may see sample pages of the eBook edition online. They do not have to purchase the eBook to preview it; the first 29 pages are open and readable. The entire work may be unlocked, read and stored on computer by completing the simple online transaction form.

Tell your friends to go to the *Are We There Yet?* Website
(http://www.awty.info)
where they may download the sample eBook edition
and explore for themselves.